AF334024
Rems
STUTTGART
EMBERG
Enz
RAUHE ALB
Lake Constance
Meersburg
KARLSRUHE
A
Baden-Baden
B L A C K
O
ORTENAU
D
E
F O R E S T
N
HINE
Offenburg
BREISGAU
FREIBURG
STRASBOURG
KAISER-
STUHL
MARKGRÄFLERLAND
Breisach
BASLE

German Wines

German Wines

by
Heinrich Meinhard

Oriel Press

First published in Great Britain 1971

© Heinrich Meinhard 1971

ISBN 0 85362 107 1

Library of Congress Catalogue Card Number 79-135981

Published by Oriel Press Limited
32 Ridley Place, Newcastle upon Tyne
England NE1 8LH

Text set in 12/13 point Bembo
Printed in Great Britain at
the Pitman Press, Bath

Contents

Illustrations

Acknowledgement

THE writer would certainly never have dreamed of writing about his experiences with German wines if his publisher-friend Bruce Allsopp had not planted the idea in his head. He dedicates this booklet to him and to all those friends, both—this country and in Germany, with whom he had the pleasure of drinking good wine.

Preface

Books on wine are, as a rule, written either by professionals in the science of oenology (wine-making) or by leading members of the wine-trade. The present writer is neither. He is an amateur, but one of many years' standing, with the experience of more than two dozen long journeys, both before and after the war, through all German wine-growing districts between the river Ahr in the north and Lake Constance in the south.

There are three English books to which he owes a great deal and which he recommends for more detailed information, viz., Frank Schoonmaker's *German Wines* (Oldbourne), 1957; Alfred Langenbach's *German Wines and Vines* (Vista Books), 1962; and S. F. Hallgarten's *Rhineland-Wineland* (Arlington Books), 4th ed., 1965. The number of German books, booklets and pamphlets on wine is legion, and a bibliography would seem to be futile. For the purpose of this Guide it may be sufficient to pick out three. Ernst Vogt's *Der Wein*, Stuttgart (Ulmer), 5th ed., 1968, is a standard work mainly on cellar technology. Among popular books, Rudolf Krämer-Badoni's *Das kleine Buch vom Wein*, Gütersloh (Bertelsmann), 2nd ed., 1968, is based on the substantial knowledge of a connoisseur of all European wines (about one-third of the book deals with non-German wines), and at the same time written in a pleasantly lively style which is mercifully free from the rhapsodical-whimsical jargon that mars so many popular German books and articles on the subject. Lastly, Heinz-Gert Woschek's *Der deutsche Weinführer*, München (Moderne

Verlagsanstalt), 1970, is a reliable guide partly based on official data. Its author, head of the *Deutsche Wein-Information* in Mainz, has been good enough to provide some of his excellent photographs for reproduction in this booklet.

The German standard work on the history of viticulture and vinification, Friedrich Basserman-Jordan's *Geschichte des Weinbaus*, 3 vols, Frankfurt, 1907, 2nd ed., 1923, has long been out of print; in this country it is not even represented among the seven million books of the British Museum Library.

There are many German professionals from whose oral information and/or publications the writer has greatly profited, more than, for reasons of space, he can name. But he wishes at least to thank his wife, who doggedly accompanied him on dozens of wine-trips and thousands of tastings and who, although she must at times have found it difficult to muster enough patience with his near-monomaniacal pursuits, never complained, at least not to him.

Finally, the reader is warned that he will find nothing in this Guide about '*Blue Nun*', '*Liebfraumilch*', '*Moselblümchen*', '*Klosterprinz*' and other '*Prinz*' wines, '*Goldener Oktober*', or any kind of branded wines with fancy names. The last named, which seems already well established on the British market, is produced as a side-line of a Bavarian dairy firm, *Allgäuer Alpenmilch*.

Commercial wines are often pushed very hard, the brashness of the advertising technique veiled behind a tone of benign fatherly advice, with a lot of pseudo-poetical verbiage about the manufacturer's unequalled understanding of soil, grapes and weather and the skill and dedication of his staff, all one big happy family, but silent about the sugaring and blending that is necessary for producing a standardized drink. At any rate, all these supermarket 'plonks' are the products of the wine-trade rather than of wine-growing, and it is to the trade that the reader should address himself for a book telling him all about them. It could be very interesting, but not to the wine-lover. Good wines are scarce and need no advertising. One has to seek them out. As the old English proverb warns us, a good wine needs no bush!

1. 𝕴ntroduction

OF ALL the wine-producing countries of Europe, and for that matter of the world, Germany is the most northerly. This simple fact determines its total acreage of viticulture, and the amount of yield,[1] which are very modest in comparison with those of the great wine-producing countries of Europe. To confine ourselves to western Europe, the French total surface planted with vines is about eighteen times that of Germany, the Italian twenty-four times, the Spanish about twenty-three times, the Portuguese about five times. The difference in extent is, however, marginally compensated for by the fact that the average German acre is far more densely planted with vines, and produces a correspondingly higher yield than that of any other country.[2] If in spite of its limited production Germany can export wines, or at least some of them, to a hundred or more countries—most of it being taken by Britain and the United States, it may have something to do with the fact that, by and large, the Germans are no great wine-drinkers. A list of annual wine-consumption in ten wine-producing countries of our continent is headed by France, while Germany figures at the bottom; per head of population the French drink between eight and nine times as much as the Germans.[3] Indeed the ratio would be a good deal more if we compared French wine consumed in France with German wine consumed in Germany. Of the total of German consumption, well above a third consists of wines imported from abroad.

Obviously, only the climatically most favoured parts of Germany are suitable for vine cultivation; that is to say, the valleys of the Rhine and its tributaries between Basle and the Siebengebirge (the 'Seven Hills') south of Bonn, to which may be added a very small area on the northern shore of Lake Constance (Bodensee in German). These valleys have the highest average temperatures, the longest summers and the shortest winters, and a rainfall which in quantity and annual distribution is most beneficial to the vines. Where sloping vineyards are immediately adjacent to rivers, or, say, Lake Constance, the water surface reflects and intensifies the sunlight and increases the moisture of the air by evaporation, both effects favouring growth and ripening of the grapes.

German wines differ from those grown in more southern countries not only by their relatively low alcoholic content but primarily by their often exquisite fragrance reminiscent of fruit or flowers, their body full of character and their pleasing after-taste, the '*Schwanz*' (tail), as it may be locally called. In the warmer countries viticulture is possible on flat ground. The German climate restricts it mainly to hilly country, gentle or even steep slopes. Its upper limit, which is reached above Lake Constance, is between 1300 and 1500 feet. Plots situated about half-way up a slope usually produce the best yield. A gradient of between fifteen degrees and thirty degrees is claimed to be the best. Obviously, a directly southern aspect provides the most favourable exposure to the sun. Slopes facing south-west and south-east are said to be the natural limits, sites facing due west or due east being, as a rule, no longer suitable for vine cultivation. Now, these last sentences are quotes from official data which are no doubt authentic in a general sense. But the traveller may often enough come across local exceptions to the general rule. For instance, he may be assured by an experienced producer in the Moselle valley that a gradient of forty degrees provides the optimal exposure to the sun. Or he may find, especially in a hot climate as that of the Kaiserstuhl (pronounced Kaizerstool) hills of southern Baden, that a great many vineyards indeed do face due west or even due east. On the other hand, as concerns gradient, to assume that the very steep slopes of the Middle Rhine must produce a better wine than the gentle ones of the neighbouring Rheingau would be a very bad guess. There are a great many factors that determine the quality of a wine.

Under the warmer sun of southern Europe the grapes ripen early, being harvested already in September, and produce sweeter and heavier wines. In the German wine-regions vines obviously do not as a rule receive as much sunlight as in the warmer countries, but in return for it the more temperate climate allows the grapes a far longer growing and ripening period; grape-gathering extends into November and occasionally even into early December. Thus the vines of Germany are given a much longer time to nourish the grapes from the minerals of the soil. These soils are very different in composition, and together with climatic differences they produce wines of a very great range of diversity. Vines can be transplanted, but soil and climate are immovables. The interaction of specific vine varieties, soil and climate produces wines which are unique and inimitable.

In English popular usage a distinction is made between Hocks and Moselles. The former designation, unknown in Germany, is a corruption of the name of the little town of Hochheim, near Wiesbaden, which came into use during the latter half of the nineteenth century. Queen Victoria, who in 1850 paid a visit to this town while taking the waters of a spa in the Taunus Hills, was presented with a small cask of the town's best wine, named in her honour *'Hochheimer Königin Victoria-Berg Riesling Auslese'*. The Queen is said to have relished the wine and to have introduced it to the palace household; and soon the abbreviated 'Hock' became the designation of any Rhine wine, and even, to judge from *The Concise Oxford Dictionary*, of German white wine generally. The name replaced the older collective one of *'Bagrag'*, a mutilation of the name of the town Bacharach on the Middle Rhine, which in earlier times served as a reloading port for all shipments from higher up the river, since the dangerous currents of the Binger Loch (Bingen gorge) could only be negotiated by smaller vessels. Another English archaism is 'Rhenish wine', but this geographical designation would of course also include the wines of Alsace and of the northern cantons of Switzerland. So we might as well settle for 'Hock' in its wider sense, lumping all German white wines together. A separate classification of Moselles ignores the fact that the wines from other tributaries of the Rhine are as distinctive in flavour and taste as are those from the Moselle, and that even the wines from different stretches of the Rhine valley are widely different in character. However, the distinction between 'Hock' and 'Moselle' may be a convenient simplification for the wine trade, since apart from the latter and those from restricted parts of the Rhine valley very few other German wines are as yet exported. Occasionally, one even reads now the designation 'red Hock', which seems to be taking simplification a bit too far.

2. A Little History

BOTH in ancient Greece and Italy wine-growing dates back beyond any historical records, and one may reasonably expect it to have reached south-eastern Gaul by about 600 B.C. with the Greek settlers who founded Massilia (Marseilles). However, it does not seem to have advanced northward to any great extent during the centuries preceding the Roman conquest. Substantially it was the Romans who transmitted viticulture to the transalpine countries. In earlier times itinerant tradesmen from Italy bartered their home-grown produce to the Celtic and Germanic barbarians, thereby also spreading its Latin name. Tacitus tells us that the Germanic tribes on the right bank of the Rhine bartered wine from foreign traders. This is likely to have been a luxury which only wealthy chiefs could afford. On the other hand, according to Caesar, the Celtic Nervii and the Germanic Suevi prohibited the import of wine on the grounds that it was a means of undermining their warlike strength. But whatever the initial reaction, the wine-trader was eventually followed by viticulture proper wherever Roman *dominium* became established.

Until about the turn of the Christian era, there seems to have been little progress in the northward expansion of viticulture in Gaul; the import of Italian wines still exceeded home production. However, the agricultural authors Columella and Pliny make it clear that at their time (about the middle of the first century A.D. or a little later) Gaul was already an independent wine-producing country rivalling Italy, planting its own varieties of vine and even exporting to Italy.

No Roman writer tells us when and by which way viticulture first entered the Rhine basin. But it obviously reached there by either or both of two ways. It may have spread to the upper Rhine via the gap between the Vosges and the Jura mountains ('la trouée de Belfort') to what is now Alsace, the Palatinate, Rhine-Hesse, and farther north along the middle Rhine, as well as to stretches on the right bank of the Rhine. Or it may be that the Moselle valley was the gate through which it spread to the Rhine. And it seems also clear that this happened no later than the second century A.D. But it should be remembered that the early wine-growers of the Rhine basin were not people of Germanic stock but more or less Romanized Celts.

Viticulture is believed to have been established in the Moselle valley in the second century A.D. The city of Trier had already been founded under Augustus, about 15 B.C., named Augusta Treverorum after the local Celtic tribe of the Treveri. The place soon became the most important rear base for the Rhine armies. But it seems that a strong indigenous economy with a flourishing trade developed only from the second century. Striking evidence of the prosperity of the valley may be found in a large number of stone sculptures, mostly in relief, dating from the late second and the first half of the third century and known as the 'Neumagen finds'. The originals are now in the Landesmuseum in Trier, but replicas of some that could be restored may be found in the village itself, which is about twenty miles down the river. They are grave-monuments, but expressing an almost humorous realism in illustrating scenes of the ordinary daily life of apparently well-to-do people. The sculptures owe their preservation to the paradox that under Constantine the Romans erected a fort at Neumagen and strengthened its walls by somewhat irreverently enclosing the local grave-monuments within them. The largest of them is that of a no-doubt wealthy wine-merchant, a galley sculptured in the round, stem and stern drawn up in the form of dog-like monsters, with a cargo of large wine-casks, rowed by a dozen oarsmen, with a helmsman at the stern and another man at the bow. There are two more grave-monuments in the form of wine-galleys in the museum, but both fragmentary; one of them is especially notable for the happiness of its helmsman's slightly befuddled grin (Plate 1).

Mosellanians take pride in a Latin poem entitled *Mosella*, dated 371, which bears witness to the venerable age of their vine-cultivation and pays tribute to the charm of their countryside. At the time Treveris, as Trier was now more briefly called, was for several decades the imperial residence of the Western Empire. The author of the poem, a man of letters named Ausonius, a native of Bordeaux, had been invited by the emperor Valentinianus to be the tutor of his son Gratianus, and he stayed on at the court under the latter's reign. The *Mosella* describes his journey from Bingen to Trier, the last stretch, from Neumagen, by boat. The river scenery reminds him of that of his native Garonne, where his own vineyard is mirrored in the light of the water surface. The *Mosella* does not seem to be rated among the gems of Latin poetry, but it has its merits as the oldest literary evidence in praise of an attractive, peaceful and apparently affluent river valley and its vine-clad hillsides in the last century of provincial Roman civilization.

The Rhine valley cannot boast monumental archaeological evidence nor any literary reference to viticulture during the period of Roman occupation, as counterparts to the Neumagen finds and to Ausonius. However, there is ample archæological evidence in the form of Roman vineyard tools, especially sickle-shaped pruning and reaping knives and two-pronged hoes. In addition, large quantities of Roman earthenware and glass vessels of various shapes for preserving and drinking wine have been brought to light. Most of this kind of evidence is to be found in the museums of Speyer, Mainz and Cologne (Plate 2).

If wine-growing took some time in establishing itself along the Moselle and Rhine, it may have something to do with the lack of official encouragement. Indeed, Rome wanted to protect home production and consequently looked upon wine-growing in the outlying provinces with a wary eye. The first reference to a decree prohibiting the cultivation of vines and olives by the transalpine peoples is by Cicero (first century B.C.). That in practice it proved to be utterly futile is proved by Columella's and Pliny's references to the flourishing vine cultivation of Gaul in the first century A.D. already mentioned.

Later we hear that the emperor Domitianus (81–96 A.D.) ordered the destruction of most of the vineyards outside Italy, an order which of course again could not be put into effect. At any rate, prohibitions were officially provoked under the emperor Probus (276–282) who, according to his biographer, 'from now on permitted all the Gauls and the Spaniards as well as the Britons to have vines and to prepare wine'.[4]

It is an often repeated commonplace that the Romans were the tutors of the Germans in the cultivation of the vine. This is true in the general sense that the Romans transmitted viticulture to the transalpine countries, not in the sense that from the beginnings of their contact Germanic-speaking people were the viticultural pupils of Roman colonists literally and directly. It was no doubt very largely from adjacent, later subjected and eventually absorbed Romanized Celts as mediators that the Germans learned the skills of wine-growing. For most of the five centuries of Roman rule, the Rhine was the frontier of the Empire, and the Rhine was also, broadly speaking, the border between Germanic and Celtic populations, though along its upper reaches people of Celtic stock extended far to the east of it. We know from both Caesar and, about a hundred and fifty years later, Tacitus that the mainstay of Germanic economy was cattle husbandry, that a rough kind of agriculture existed but that the Germans did not care for it very much, that fruit trees and generally horticulture were nonexistent. Moreover, at least in the turbulent conditions before and during Caesar's time, when most of the Germanic peoples moved, in intermittent and slow migrations, westward and southward in search of new land, agriculture was more or less itinerant; the tribes cultivated during intervals between expansionist movements. They were not nomadic in the true sense, but neither were they sedentary. However, the cultivation of vines, which bear their first grapes only after a number of years, and equally that of any fruit trees demands an absolutely stable and sedentary way of life.

The question at what time people of Germanic speech first laboured in their vineyards with their own hands, or at least came to own vineyards, cannot, of course, be answered with any certainty. At first sight it seems to be pretty late. On the whole, sedentariness, the prerequisite of viticulture, never seems to have lasted very long among the Germans during the period of Roman rule. In the second half of the third century, bands of Alemannic and Frankish[5] warriors breached the frontier, launching an invasion of Gaul and sacking Trier in 275/6. The emperor Probus (276–282), who eventually threw them back across the Rhine, significantly omits to mention the Germans as wine-growers in his famous edict (see above, p. 10).

At the beginning of the fifth century, Roman rule on the left bank of the Rhine came to an end. At this time Alemannians and Ripuarian Franks (*viz.*, riverain Franks, from Latin *ripa*, riverbank) definitely settled on the left bank, at first apparently still nominally recognizing Roman sovereignty. From about the middle of the fifth century, when Roman rule in Gaul was crumbling, Salian Franks from the lower Rhine occupied northern Gaul, thereafter conquering successively one part after the other of the country; the Ripuarian Franks occupied the country to the west of the middle Rhine; at about the same time, the Alemannians completed the occupation of the left bank of the upper Rhine, the present Rhine-Hesse, the Palatinate, Alsace and a large part of Switzerland, while retaining their older seats on the eastern side of the river, the Odenwald and Black Forest areas. A few decades later, they overreached themselves in their attempt to expand northward at the expense of the Ripuarians, which ended in 496 with their defeat by Clovis, the first king of the Merovingian dynasty. They paid for it by being expelled from the northern half of their territories, which were now being occupied by Frankish settlers, and by having to recognize the suzerainty of the Frankish kings. One outcome of the Frankish victory was their christianization, followed by that of the defeated Alemannians. Apart from making them more acceptable to their Christian Gallo-Roman subjects, their conversion is also likely to have been of some influence on the future development of viticulture (see below, p. 15).

It might well be asked where and when in these turbulent centuries could people of Germanic speech have attained that state of stable and lasting sedentariness that is indispensable to viticulture. And one would come to the conclusion that the beginnings of a lasting German viticulture cannot be dated, at the earliest, before the second half of the fifth century, when the Romans had finally left, and that the Germans learnt the skills of viticulture not from Roman masters, but from the remaining Romanized Celts who had become their subject population and later amalgamated with them.

Yet there are some clues pointing to much earlier beginnings of genuine German viticulture, whether lasting or short-lived, as well as to a more immediate Roman-German relationship in the matter. The main point in favour of this assumption is the influx, in ever-increasing numbers since the third century, of Germanic elements into the Roman military service and agricultural labour force in Gaul. The semi-servile Germanic peasant communities, partly prisoners of war from various tribes or their descendants, seem to have made up a sizeable proportion of the population of Gaul. It stands to reason that some of them must have been vineyard-labourers. After the conquest of Gaul by the Franks, these Germanic bondsmen and ex-legionaries were admitted to the status of free Franks. The *Lex Salica* (*c.* 500), the law-book of the Frankish conquerors of Gaul, takes the familiarity with an old-established viticulture already for granted.

The Roman influence on German vine cultivation is evident from the substantial number of surviving Latin loan-words in its nomenclature. German *Wein* (wine) is of course derived from Latin *vinum*; this word, already picked up from the early Roman wine-peddlers, percolated as a loan-word even into all the Baltic and Slavonic languages. German *Winzer* (wine-grower) is derived from *vinitor*; *Most* (must) from *mustum*; *Keller* (cellar) from *cellarium*; *Kufe* (cask, coop) from *cupa*; *Küfer* (cooper) from *cuparius*; *Kelch* (cup, goblet; in ecclesiastical language, chalice) from *calix*. Of special interest are a few loan-words in German which are not, or at any rate no longer, represented in French and therefore also absent in English. The word *Trichter* (funnel) is derived from *trajectorium*. The noun *Kelter* (wine-press), with the verb *keltern*, is derived from *calcatorium*, a derivative of the verb *calcare*, to tread upon or underfoot. Another word denoting a wine-press, but restricted to the upper Rhine area, is *Torkel*, from *torcular* or *torculum*, a press. The application of the loan-word *Kelter* to a press appears to be based on a misunderstanding. The Latin word *calcatorium* means nothing more than a raised platform on which the treaders, *calcatores*, crushed the grapes with their bare feet. On the other hand, the Latin *torcular* or *torculum*, from which *Torkel* is derived, actually denotes a press. Such presses are known from descriptions by Roman writers and from wall-paintings at Pompeii and Herculaneum. The most primitive contraption consisted of a heavy block of stone lifted by a long wooden lever-beam and lowered on to a basket containing the grapes. More developed specimens operated by the pressure of a heavy beam, and they in their turn became old-fashioned after the invention of a screw-press, a smaller machine that could be operated without the inconvenience of the long lever press-beam.[6] The German word *Presse* is rarely used in connection with traditional wine-making, although it is of course used for modern machines.

There may have been a good many other viticultural expressions derived from Latin which, however, reached only an early stage in the development of German, then to be discarded in favour of a genuine German word. An example is the Old High-German *windemon*, derived from Latin *vindemia* (grapeharvest), the word that has also sprouted French *vendang* and English *vintage*. The early loan-word has disappeared and been replaced, in literary German, by *Weinlese* and, in the winegrower's language, by *Herbst*.

The word *Rebe* (vine) is a notable exception from the vocabulary of loan-words, but in this peculiarity it has a Latin parallel. The Latin *vinea*, derived from *vinum*, is ambiguous in that it means both vine and vineyard. In the first sense it is synonymous with *vitis*. In English, the words viniculture (from *vinum*) and viticulture (from *vitis*) are synonymous. But *vitis* is alliterative with *vinum* only by chance; etymologically the two words are unrelated. The basic meaning of *vitis* is 'something that winds about', a pliant, flexible plant, a creeper. The German word *Rebe*, appears to have the same meaning; it may have been applied to other kinds of winding plant before it was reserved for the vine.

There is also a good deal of Latin debris surviving in names of vineyard sites, especially on the Moselle, e.g., Calmont probably from *calidus mons* (hot hill) or possibly from *calvus mons* (bald hill); Cramunt from *gradalis mons* (hill in the form of steps); Monteneubel from *mons nobilis* (famous hill), etc.

Coming back to *Winzer*, one often finds it rendered, even in books written by leading members of the wine-trade, by the English 'vintner'. What the two words have in common is that they have something to do with wine, and that they alliterate. They are different both in meaning and derivation. A vintner is of course a wine-merchant, the word being derived from the Old French *vinetier*, now extinct, which goes back to Late Latin *vinetarius*, which again has replaced *vinarius* of classical Latin. The Winzer is a wine-grower, although the expression is normally restricted to the smallholder; the word is derived from the Latin *vinitor* which has the same meaning, but more specifically that of a vineyard slave. The name of the Moselle village Wintrich is derived from a Celto-Roman *Vinitoriacum*, meaning wine-growers' village. There is an English word vintager meaning grape-gatherer, which does not seem to crop up very often in either speech or print, but it means no more than someone who lends a helpful hand with the vintage. Many British and American soldiers, erroneously hoping this activity to be attended by romantic accompaniments, have been welcome helpers in German grape-harvests, but it is a moot question whether they realized that they were vintagers. At any rate, a vintager, or grape-gatherer, is not a Winzer, or grape-grower, who toils in the vineyard all the year round.

The long and violent period of Germanic migrations and land-grabbing does not appear to have been as destructive to viticulture as might be expected. A relatively peaceful continuation of vine-cultivation under Frankish rule appears to be borne out by passages from the Merovingian law-books, the *Lex Salica* (*c.* 500) and the *Lex Ripuaria* (from about the end of the sixth century). The former reveals its regard for vine-cultivation by raising the social status of the grower, though still servile, above that of the common ploughman, and consequently by fixing the blood-compensation payable for the slaying of a vineyard labourer considerably above that laid down for the slaying of a mere agricultural serf. The law of the Ripuarian Franks, in a paragraph indicating the formalities attending conveyances, suggests, by the wording 'a country-estate, or a vineyard, or any small piece of land', that vineyards were a common form of immovable property.

A more or less undisturbed transition from the Roman to the Frankish period is also evident from a second description of the Moselle scenery, two centuries after Ausonius' *Mosella*, showing that vine-cultivation was again flourishing as vigorously as it had been under Roman rule. It is a poetic itinerary of a river journey, composed by Venantius Fortunatus, a scholarly cleric and the last Latin poet of his time. For some time he lived at the Austrasian court at Metz under the rule of Sigibert and his successor Childe-bert. The poem, written to commemorate a river-trip in 588, has an additional significance in that it not only praises the vine-clad hillsides of the Moselle, but also refers to extensive vineyards near Andernach, about ten miles down the Rhine from Koblenz.

If the cultivation of the vine escaped the worst of the depreda-tions during the period of the Germanic invasions, it is no doubt also in a large measure due to its protection by the Christian Church, which actively propagated it. The essential root of the ecclesiastical concern with viticulture is the fact that wine is an irreplaceable element in the celebration of the Eucharist, the central sacrament of the Christian religion, which is founded on the doctrine of transubstantiation, the miraculous conversion of the consecrated bread and wine into the flesh and blood of Christ. The heathen Germans used to cheer or fuddle their brains with mead, grain fermented with honey; if the mead-swillers were to be brought into the Church, wine had to be available. Naturally, it was also required by the monasteries for ordinary non-sacral use; monks received their daily rations, the aged and sick had to be comforted, pilgrims to be regaled, etc.

The mystical vision of the divine treader of grapes, 'Christ in the wine-press' (Plate 3), appears to be an offshoot of the conception of the Eucharist as a memorial of the Passion. The image of Christ is seen standing in the tub of the press, bent under the cross which is pressed down on his back by the screw of the press, his blood flowing from his side and hands and mingling with the grape-juice. This symbol has a varied imagery: in simple sculptures in vineyard-shrines, in stone reliefs (the best-known example in the vineyard chapel overlooking the little town of Ediger on the Moselle), in more elaborate paintings, etc. There are various references to it in early Christian writings, the earliest apparently in those of St. Augustine (c. 400): 'The first cluster of the vine to be pressed in the wine-press is Christ'.[7]

In the early Middle Ages, Charlemagne (742–814) is on record for his active encouragement of viticulture. He is credited with setting up model estates, each of which had to have its own wine-shop displaying a wreath of vine-leaves—a custom still surviving in the 'Strausswirtschaften' (wreath-inns) or 'Heckenwirtschaften' (hedge-inns), wine-growers' cottages marked in the same same way, where the owner can legally sell his own produce. (An echo of this is the English proverb, *a good wine needs no bush*.) Some of Charlemagne's feats in promoting viticulture are a little apocryphal. An old story, very dear to the Rheingau people, is that the emperor, from his palace at Ingelheim on the other side of the Rhine, noticed that the snow on the wooded slopes opposite melted much earlier than elsewhere, concluded that they received an extra dose of sunshine, and immediately ordered them to be cleared and planted with vines. However, there may well be some truth behind the legend, for the first historical document mentioning the existence of a vineyard in the Rheingau, issued by the emperor's son Louis the Pious, is dated 817, three years after Charlemagne's death. This is indeed late in comparison with documentary evidence of viticulture on the upper Rhine. Rheingau viticulture on any substantial scale can only be traced back to the twelfth century, being associated with the foundation of the Benedictine monastery of Johannisberg and the installation of the first batch of Cistercian monks in the Eberbach monastery by St. Bernard of Clairvaux.

Since the Carolingian period, local rulers and aristocratic magnates owned large slices of vineyard sites, but it seems that an even larger part came, through donations and bequests, royal or otherwise, into the possession of the Church. The monasteries especially were the pioneers in the expansion of viticulture. Between the tenth and twelfth centuries monks had already established vineyards in Saxony, Thuringia, and Brandenburg; in the fifteenth they had spread them virtually everywhere in northern Germany, even beyond the Vistula to East Prussia. The extension of viticulture to a northern climate inhospitable to the vine can only be explained from ecclesiastical requirements. For ordinary consumption the thin and sour wines grown in those parts were sweetened with honey, spiced and mulled.

In the sixteenth century the Hanseatic League imported sweeter and stronger wines, mainly from France and southern Europe, which ousted the inferior northern product. From southern Germany, during the same time, we hear of occasional vintages so plentiful that considerable problems of storage arose. Old chronicles record harvests when last year's wine had to be poured into the streets to make casks available for the new one.

Such abundance came to an end during the Thirty Years' War (1618–1648), which everywhere laid waste immense vineyard areas, destroying the wine-trade as well. Vine cultivation in north and east Germany as well as in southern Bavaria never recovered from its ravages. By the end of the seventeenth century what remained of viticulture had, more or less, retreated to its older homeland, the climatically favoured valleys of the Rhine and its tributaries. Together with the withdrawal from unfavourable regions, a gradual but very drastic shrinkage of viticultural acreage ensued in the remaining wine-growing regions. Vines planted on more or less level ground had to give way to corn and other crops, in accordance with a general rule saying 'Where a plough can go there no vine should grow'. The wine-producing acreage about the year 1600 is estimated to have been *c.* 300,000 hectares, that remaining today is just 72,000. These changes signal the first beginnings of a gradual switch-over from quantitative to qualitative production. The principal obstacle to improvement was the unfortunate social position of the tenant smallholder, who was heavily burdened with rents and taxes as well as with the wine-tithe enforced by the Church, and who was therefore mainly interested in mass-production, planting varieties producing a massive yield of inferior quality. Nevertheless, during the second half of the eighteenth century some qualitative improvement was achieved, due in a large measure to the efforts of the two Rheingau monasteries of Johannisberg and Eberbach; more promising sites were planted with better varieties, cellar methods were improved, wines bottled and wine-labels introduced. On the other hand, some happy-go-lucky old methods continued for a while, such as the 'mixed setting', or higgledy-piggledy planting of different kinds of vine on the same plot in spite of the different ripening time of their grapes. This has been eliminated only since the middle of the nineteenth century and replaced by the 'pure setting', the careful segregation of different kinds of vine not only on separate plots, but wherever possible also on different kinds of soil best suited to promote their growth and to benefit yield and quality of their grapes.

The nineteenth century began with a severe setback to viticulture, namely, the secularization of 1803, by which the Church was dispossessed of its entire landed property. This meant that many centuries of devoted monastic labour, not motivated by commercial interests, had come to an end. The vineyards hitherto owned by the monasteries and other ecclesiastical institutions were partly appropriated by various secular rulers, later to become the nucleus of the present 'State Domains', but the bulk was sold to private producers, from large titled landowners to more humble wine-growers, as well as to the wine-trade.

There is a vast number of site-names, to be found on wine-labels after the local name, referring to erstwhile possession by monasteries, nunneries, cathedrals, parish churches, etc. The best-known is perhaps that of the celebrated Forster Jesuitengarten in the Palatinate. They crop up with a particular density on the Moselle, for example, Domdechaney, Domherrenberg, Bischofs-berg, Abteiberg, Abtsberg, Mönchsberg, Pfaffenberg, Bruder-schaft, Nonnenberg, Nonnenlay, Frauenberg, Juffer (=Jungfer, Jungfrau, meaning virgin, an epithet restricted to nuns in this context), Pastorat, Kirchenstück, and other specimens of the kind.

3. The Vines

THE STUDY of vines, as a branch of botany, is known as ampelography (from *ampelos*, the Greek word for the plant). Of the various factors that determine the character of a wine, the foremost is, naturally, the kind of vine from the grapes of which it is produced. German production consists of eighty-five per cent white and fifteen per cent red wines. According to the latest available statistics,[8] the respective share of the principal varieties in the total of the vine-planted surface is as follows: White: *Silvaner* twenty-five per cent, *Riesling* twenty-four per cent, *Müller-Thurgau* twenty-four per cent, *Ruländer* three per cent, *Morio-Muskat* two per cent. Red: *Portugieser* seven per cent. *Blauer Spätburgunder* (Blue Late Burgundy) three per cent, *Trollinger* two per cent. Other varieties (both white and red and including good, bad and indifferent): ten per cent. There is a considerable variability in the proportion of kinds of vine planted in different wine-growing regions, primarily determined by the prevailing kind of soil. There is also a good deal of variability in the character of wine made from the same kind of vine but grown in different regions, again depending mainly on the kind of soil.

Riesling

To begin with the second of the list, the international reputation of German wine is chiefly based on the Riesling (pronounced *Reesling*), indisputably the queen of all German vines and, other things being equal, producing a wine unsurpassed in fragrance by any other white wine anywhere. The Riesling belongs essentially to the northern boundary of the wine-growing zone and produces a greater variety of distinguished wines, each with a specific local character of its own, than any other kind of vine. It is represented in all wine-growing regions of Germany, though in very different proportions, from about eighty or more per cent in the Moselle region, the Middle Rhine and the Rheingau down to a mere three or four per cent in Franconia. It is believed to be native to the Rhine valley, a descendant of a Rhenish wild strain, but on the whole it seems to have remained unsegregated and unrecognized for centuries in the 'mixed settings' of the past, till eventually its superior qualities were appreciated. However, recent research has shown that it was known, at least locally, in the fifteenth century, the oldest known record mentioning the name being dated 1435. If the Riesling vine is not planted more extensively, the reason is that it is among the most demanding of German vines in respect of soil, site, climate and grower's care. On the whole, it prefers steep hillsides and stony ground; although hardier against frost it is more sensitive to wind than other varieties; its grapes are small-berried and among the last to ripen, exposing them to greater weather risks. It does not like too hot or too dry weather; for example, Riesling wines of the hot and dry Kaiserstuhl in southern Baden, otherwise a veritable 'Bacchus' kitchen', are a little disappointing when compared with those of the Rheingau or other more northern parts. It is indeed grown in Alsace, which geographically is a Rhenish country, but not in any other part of France.

What, then, about more southern wines known by such names as South Tyrolese Riesling, Hungarian Riesling, Banat Riesling, Yugoslav Riesling, etc.? They are worthy enough wines, but all most of them have in common with the true Riesling vine is the fact that they trade on the cachet of its name. Ampelographers distinguish the genuine vine as 'White Riesling' from various local strains collectively known as 'Welschriesling'. (The word 'Welsch', now obsolete in ordinary use, means foreigner, in this case denoting the Romance-speaking neighbours of the Germans, both French and Italian; compare the more-restricted English use of 'Welsh' for Celtic-speaking neighbours.) The leaves of the Welschriesling are different in form from those of the White Riesling and the grapes bigger and darker in colour; the vine is generally richer in yield and produces good table-wines, which however lack the fragrance and the fruity and spicy taste of the genuine White Riesling. In German use, the word Riesling invariably means White Riesling only, because no Welschriesling is grown. On the other hand, in countries in which both kinds of vine are planted, the sole and indiscriminate use of the name Riesling to cover both is apt to cause confusion, to say the least.

Silvaner

As regards quantity, the Silvaner (also spent Sylvaner) heads the roster of German vines. Proportionally, its cultivation is highest in Franconia with between forty-eight and fifty per cent, rather high in Rhine-Hesse, the Palatinate and the Nahe valley with forty-one, thirty-five and thirty-three per cent respectively, low in the Rheingau with eight per cent, in Baden with seven per cent and on the Middle Rhine with four per cent, while the Moselle with its tributaries Saar and Ruwer as well as farther north the Ahr valley do not grow any Silvaner. Synonyms of the name are Österreicher (Austrian), by which it is known in the Rheingau, and which may possibly indicate the direction from which it was introduced, and Frankentraube (Franconian grape), used in the Palatinate. On the whole, Silvaner wines cannot match Rieslings. Their bouquet is more neutral, though they may have a light fragrance; the taste is generally broader, softer and milder, though in good vintages, and when grown on suitable soils, it may be full-bodied, fruity and of an agreeable sweetness. After all, not every wine-drinker favours a wine with a very distinctive bouquet; some are happier with a mellow one. Indeed, the best years produce Silvaner wines of highest quality. The reason why this vine is planted so widely is that it is less exacting in its demands on climate and soil, often contenting itself with heavy soils where Riesling would fail, that it is more prolific, with a higher yield

Plate 1. The happy helmsman. Detail from a Roman grave-monument showing a wine-ship found at Neumagen; Landesmuseum, Trier.

Plate 2 (above). Almost fully restored Roman grave monument showing a wine-ship found at Neumagen; Landesmuseum, Trier.

Plate 2 (below). Roman wine vessels found in the Palatinate. Wine Museum in the Historisches Museum der Pfalz, Speyer.

Plate 3 (above). Eberbach Monastery in the Rheingau.
Photo by courtesy of the Director, Hesse State Domains.

Plate 3 (below). Christ in the Wine-press. Painting on wood in Johannisberg Castle.
Photo by courtesy of the Manager.

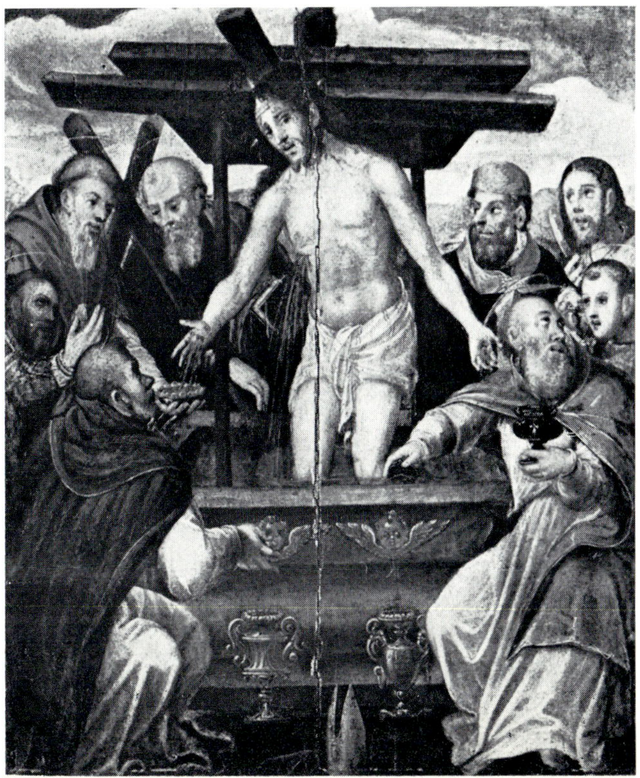

Plate 4. Planting a young vine.
Photo by courtesy of Deutsche Wein-Information, Mainz.

Plate 5. Vine blossom.
Photo by courtesy of Deutsche Wein-Information, Mainz.

Plate 6 (above). Blue Late Burgundy and white Müller-Thurgau grapes in a Kaiserstuhl vineyard.

Plate 6 (below). Zeltingen on the Moselle river.

Plate 7. The writer with local friends in a Kaiserstuhl vineyard.

Plate 8 (above). The Mondhalde site between Oberrotweil and Oberbergen in the Kaiserstuhl, with new terraces in the foreground.

Plate 8 (below). St. Goarshausen with the castled crag of Burg Katz (Cat Castle), Middle Rhine.

Photographs by courtesy of Deutsche Wein-Information, Mainz.

to the acre, generally more reliable, and that its grapes ripen earlier. On the other hand, it is more sensitive to frost than Riesling.

Müller-Thurgau

The Müller-Thurgau vine, also labelled Riesling x Silvaner (the first name after its Swiss breeder who developed it in the Geisenheim Institute in 1882, the second identifying it as a crossing between the two principal varieties), matches Riesling in total distribution and is, in varying proportions, represented in all German wine-growing regions. Its popularity with growers is due to the fact that it is modest in its claims on climate and soil, often being planted on very slightly sloping or even flat and heavy ground just above the valley bottom, and that it is very prolific and early ripening. Its wines are mostly light and fresh, with a pleasant bouquet, mild acidity, and a taste reminiscent of muscatel. However, they do not keep long. Though hardly in the vintage class, the Müller-Thurgau is a very successful crossing, especially qualified to supplant inferior old varieties still surviving locally. (The name 'Riesling x Silvaner', incidentally, should be distinguished from the occasionally found designation of 'Riesling und Silvaner', which has nothing to do with the hybrid vine but denotes a 50:50 blend of Riesling and Silvaner wines in the cask.) More recent crossings between Riesling and Silvaner vines are the Rieslaner (also mis-named Main Riesling) and the Scheurebe, called after its breeder, both more or less confined to Franconia and grown in small quantities.

Ruländer

One of the most distinguished of German quality wines, though limited in quantity and geographical distribution, is the Ruländer, also called Grauer Burgunder (Grey Burgundy, Pinot gris). Its main centre of cultivation is the volcanic Kaiserstuhl massif in southern Baden. It is also grown in neighbouring Alsace, where it is labelled Tokay d'Alsace. Local folklore of the upper Rhine connects it with a nobleman named Lazarus von Schwendi, a native of the Kaiserstuhl who rose to become an imperial field-commander, and who is reputed to have brought the vine from Hungary. However, ampelographically Ruländer has nothing in common with Tokay vines. If the latter name is at all used for it, it can only be justified on the grounds that the two wines are comparable in fullness and strength. A probably more authentic story connects the Ruländer vine with a merchant named Ruland, of Speyer in the Palatinate, who is said to have brought shoots from France in the early eighteenth century. In its character, Ruländer is not comparable with either Riesling or Silvaner, nor indeed with any other German wine. It is a heavy, full-bodied, even fiery wine with a high alcoholic content and delicate bouquet, which in ageing turns into a dark golden-yellow colour.

Morio-Muskat

Morio-Muskat, said in official statistics to constitute two per cent of the vine-planted surface (which from the writer's experience seems puzzlingly exaggerated), is a crossing between Weissburgunder (White Burgundy, Pinot blanc) and Silvaner, named after its breeder. It is a wine of pleasant piquancy, grown in small quantities in Rhine-Hesse and the Palatinate.

Gutedel

Among white varieties of the statistical category 'Others', the very productive Gutedel (pronounced *Gootédel*) vine is perhaps the most important; in fact, there is probably as much Gutedel planted as there is Ruländer. In Germany, it is more or less confined to the Markgräflerland, the foothills of the southern Black Forest between Freiburg and Basle. It is known to have been introduced here, about two hundred years ago, by the Margrave Karl Friedrich of Baden, from Lake Geneva, where it is known as Fendant. It is also fairly widely known in Alsatian vineyards, where its French name is Chasselas. Being the predominant variety in the Markgräflerland, the name Markgräfler has come to be a synonym of Gutedel in Germany. The wine has a delicate bouquet, is mild and of low acidity. Although not in the vintage class, wines from the best Markgräfler sites deserve better than being rated as second-class table-wines, as they often are. They are by no means all consumed locally, but have an expanding circle of adherents elsewhere in southern Germany.

Traminer

The Traminer (pronounced *Trameener*) vine, with a variant called Gewürztraminer ('aromatic' Traminer), is said to have received its name from the village of Tramin in the South Tyrol, and also to be the oldest German vine, identified already 1500 or 1600 years ago. Both claims may be accepted with reservation. Like Riesling, Traminer is exacting with regard to climate and soil, small-berried and late in ripening. Being very sensitive to weather in the blossoming season, its yield is not reliable. Most of it comes from Baden, where its main centre of cultivation is the Ortenau district opposite Strasbourg, and where its local name is Clevner. It is also planted to some extent on the Kaiserstuhl hills, in smaller quantities also elsewhere in Baden, but invariably on the best sites. It is also grown to an appreciable extent in the Palatinate and Rhine-Hesse, much less in Württemberg, while in Franconia, with its generally somewhat less favourable climate, it is a rare speciality. Traminer wines are highly appreciated because of their incomparable bouquet. Some people who find the especially strong Muscatel-like flavour of the Gewürztraminer not to their liking are apt to declare it as a 'ladies' wine'. However, in body this derivative shares the qualities of the Traminer, fullness, mellowness and high alcoholic content. These vines are planted in far greater quantities in Alsace; indeed, it is not too much to say that the high reputation of Alsatian viticulture is largely based on its excellent Traminer and Gewürztraminer wines.

Muscatel, Weissburgunder and Elbling

Muscatel and Weissburgunder (Pinot blanc) are of more restricted distribution, especially in Rhine-Hesse, the Palatinate and Baden, although it seems that the latter at least is becoming increasingly popular. But there is also a white variety with a very poor reputation skulking in the category 'Others'. This is the Elbling, also called Kleinberger (or Klemperich), or Räuschling (the latter name is also sometimes said to denote a variant), an exceedingly prolific vine producing a thin and sour wine. Its introduction is ascribed to the Romans, and the name Elbling, or in Baden locally Alben, claimed to be derived from that of an ancient Roman variety, albuelis, mentioned by the elder Pliny. However that may be, its main refuge is, or was until fairly recently, the upper Moselle along the Luxemburg border, where, apart from local consumption, it is, or was, mainly sold as a basis for cheaper Sparkling Moselle. It was also grown locally in Baden and Württemberg as late as the 1950s. It is likely that such prolific but inferior vines were the mainstay of the mass-production of past centuries. Today they are increasingly supplanted by the Müller-Thurgau vine. However, not a few people are not entirely happy with the change; they were used to the refreshing natural prickliness of the much maligned Elbling.

Red Varieties—Portugieser

Red varieties are represented mainly in the Ahr valley and in Württemberg, each with more than half, and in Baden with nearly a quarter of the total production. According to our statistics, the Portugieser vine covers the major share of the acreage planted with red varieties, seven per cent of the total vine-planted surface. This vine, whose connection with Portugal may be doubted, can be planted on almost any kind of soil, but is sensitive to frost. It is very prolific, with biggish, early-ripening grapes producing a light and mild unassuming country-wine, often somewhat low in acidity, and with either no bouquet at all or with a not very agreeable one. It is found mainly in the Palatinate, in Rhine-Hesse, in Württemberg, more sporadically in northern Baden, in Franconia, and on the less-favoured sites of the Ahr valley. Red wines without special designation are mostly Portugieser wines.

Blauer Spätburgunder

The Blue Late Burgundy (Pinot noir), covering three per cent of the total vine-planted surface, produces the best red wine to be found in Germany. It is believed that the Cistercian monks, who in the twelfth century settled in the Eberbach monastery in the Rheingau, brought the Pinot noir vine from Clairvaux and first cultivated it on the slaty slopes of the present town of Assmannshausen. An obsolete name of it is 'Klebrot'; this name, in variable older spellings, can be traced back for 500 years in Eberbach inventories and elsewhere. The vine is as demanding as the Riesling, it needs deep fertile soils retaining sufficient moisture, a sheltered situation and a warm climate with low rainfall. At the present time, Late Burgundy has its largest distribution in Baden, where it accounts for about twenty-two per cent of the total production, being mainly cultivated on well-sheltered sites of the Ortenau and in the Kaiserstuhl hills, and in the Ahr valley, where its share goes up to twenty-four per cent of the total production. In good years its wines have a very fine aroma, are full-bodied, smooth and velvety in taste and rich in alcoholic content. Obviously, the German Late Burgundy cannot, on the whole, be expected to match the quality of the French original. All the same, denigrators of the German product—and there are enough of them in Germany, too—might make some concessions after tasting Late Burgundy at its best, for example, in the Hesse State Domain at Assmannshausen.

Trollinger

The Trollinger vine, covering two per cent of the total vine-planted surface, has its main distribution in Württemberg, accounting for twenty-seven per cent of that country's total production. The name points to its introduction from the Tyrol. Its grapes ripen late and produce a wine of light-red colour, refreshing and robust in taste. It is very popular in Württemberg, and certainly superior to Portugieser. In the South Tyrol it is used for table-grapes known as Meraner Kurtraube (Meran health-grape). Synonyms of the name are Frankentaler and Blauer Malvasier (Blue Malmsey).

Blauer Frühburgunder, Schwarzriesling, Limberger and St. Laurent

Of the remaining red wines, covered by the statistical category 'Others', the most important is the Blauer Frühburgunder (Blue Early Burgundy), whose earlier-ripening grapes produce a wine lighter in alcoholic content which, although of typical Burgundy taste, rarely reaches Late Burgundy quality. Its main distribution is in Rhine-Hesse, northern Baden and western Franconia. Württemberg again has its Schwarzriesling (Black Riesling), also called Müllerrebe (Müller vine), producing a somewhat sweetish wine. Another two, planted more sporadically in Baden and Württemberg: the Limberger (or Lemberger) and the St. Laurent vines.

Weissherbst

Lastly, the Weissherbst (lit. 'White harvest'), better known in this country under its French name Rosé. This is certainly a special kind of wine, and indeed a quite important one, but it is not obtained from a special kind of vine. It may be prepared from any kind of blue grape (though the wine law narrows this down to German blue grape), but in Baden, where it is more popular than anywhere else, it is made exclusively from the Late Burgundy (Pinot noir) grape. Its difference from a red wine is caused by another method of preparation. It must be noted that the cellar treatment of red wines is somewhat different from that of white ones. The greenish-yellow grapes of the latter go more or less straight through the press after being gathered. The blue ones of the former are crushed into a mash, and this is left to stand for some time to ferment before being pressed. During this process of mash-fermentation the juice of the blue grapes, which is naturally as colourless as that of the white-skinned ones, assumes its colour, and its more astringent taste, from the tannic acid contained in the blue pigment of the grape-skins. Now the lighter colour of the Weissherbst, or Rosé, as compared with that of red wine, is due to the fact that it is not subjected to this procedure. Its red-wine grapes are pressed exactly as are white-wine grapes, that is, immediately after the gathering, and in this way they can, in fermentation, absorb only a very limited amount of tannic acid from the pigment of their skins. Normally, the colour of Weiss-herbst is the well-known lighter or darker pink. But that of the best-quality may better be described as a pale golden colour with only a slight reddish hue to it.

Pests

In the second half of the nineteenth century, German viticulture was attacked by destructive vine-pests, introduced from the United States via France, especially the fungoid *Peronospora*, which causes leaves and grapes to shrivel on the vine, *Oidium*, a kind of mildew, and, the most devastating scourge, the *Phylloxera*, called in German 'Reblaus' (vine-louse), a minute insect which feeds on the roots of vines. After long years of experimentation, the remedy was eventually found in the combination of two plants, the 'Pfropfrebe', or grafted vine, produced by the grafting of grape-bearing native vines on stems derived from *Phylloxera*-resisting roots of wild American vines. The danger of the *Phylloxera still* remains more or less dormant, but on the whole it is now under control; old-established vineyards may partly still be under non-grafted native vines, but the more recent are as a rule planted only with vines of the grafted kind.

4. Harvesting

IT MAY be useful to introduce this chapter by saying something about the subdivision of viticultural property. The word *Lage* (site) denotes a named unit of viticultural acreage, continuous in extent, relatively uniform in aspect and homogeneous in composition. As a rule, its name follows that of the locality on the label, for example, Rauenthaler Siebenmorgen or Niersteiner Zehnmorgen, both names denoting a square measure; but the name of a site may also refer to former ecclesiastical or aristocratic ownership, to natural features, etc. In the case of the Rauenthal wine, the label gives the name of the local growers' co-operative, which means that the site is split up into a great many individual holdings, all or most of the owners selling their produce to the co-operative. The label of the Nierstein wine gives the name of the producer's firm and the statement 'Lage im Alleinbesitz' (site in exclusive possession). Generally, only a small minority of sites are exclusively owned by one family, mostly with an aristocratic name, or by a State domain. The overwhelming majority of sites are subdivided into a smaller number of larger, or a larger number of smaller properties. A number of famous sites in the Rheingau belong exclusively to some or other aristocratic owner; the Steinberg site, worked for centuries by the Cistercians of the Eberbach monastery, is the exclusive property of the Hesse State domain, but in the case of the Marcobrunnen site the same domain has to share ownership with four or five aristocratic proprietors. In Baden, a country where smallholdings are the predominant feature of all agriculture, it would be difficult to find a site that is in someone's exclusive ownership.

Grapes ripen earlier or later in accordance with local climatic conditions; for instance, the main harvest in the Kaiserstuhl of southern Baden may be all over well before that on the Moselle, in the north, has even begun. Howevei, no grower anywhere is allowed to begin his grape-picking whenever he thinks fit. The beginning of the harvest is laid down by a local committee whose decision is binding on all growers. (This practice is, of course, not confined to Germany; e.g., in Bordeaux the official opening of the harvesting is a ceiemony of especial pomp and circumstance.) During a week or so before the official beginning vineyards are closed, surrounded with wire-fences; and signs are set up warning the public to keep out. This prohibition applies not only to out-siders but, perhaps less strictly, also to the owners themselves. In rainy weather, grape-picking is out of the question. In the process of grape-picking, speed and precision are essential. Grapes picked in the course of the day have to be taken to the cellar before evening to be pressed as quickly as possible. In traditional practice collected grapes were, often still in the vineyard, crushed into a mash by means of a portable grape-mill. This is still often done with more ordinary grapes, although co-operatives may object to it generally; at any rate, better-quality grapes should be delivered to the cellar in, if possible, undamaged condition to go first into a special machine which 'tops and tails' them before they are pressed.

The natural sugar, and potential alcohol, content of a must (that is, grape-juice), is ascertained from its specific gravity, already before the pressing, from a sample of the grape-mash. This is done by means of the Öchsle must-scale, a cylindrical glass device named after its inventor who developed it about a hundred and forty years ago. The scale indicates the specific gravity of the must in the shortened form of the 'Öchsle degrees', that is, the decimal figures behind the comma. For example, if the specific gravity is 1,070, the scale shows 70°, if it is 1,110 it shows 110°. Considering the average annual yield of a whole region, if it is only 60° Öchsle overall, it would be a very inferior harvest indeed; 75° to 80° would be a normal, anything above 90° a very good regional average. The individual grower may, in a good year and from a good site, get a crop showing 100° or 110° Öchsle and promising a very good wine. The top figures of 1953 and 1959 ('the wine of the century', as the latter year's product was called in Germany), referring of course to isolated cases, were 275° and 312° respectively.

However, German viticulture is, of course, always subject to the unpredictabilities of a northern climate. There are good, bad and middling years. Of the post-war years, the greatest vintages were 1945, 1947, 1949, 1953, 1959 and 1964. In a year with poor sunshine and too much rain, when grapes do not mature fully, some or most musts do not reach the required specific gravity, that is, the natural sugar content revealing a satisfactory alcoholic potential, or they may suffer from an excess of acidity. Such musts have to be artificially sweetened to produce a potable wine of normal alcoholic content. This practice, incidentally, is by no means confined to German wine-making, but may also be found in France and elsewhere. In Germany, it is known by the term 'verbessern' (to improve), or, more occasionally, 'anreichern' (to enrich), both of course euphemisms for sugaring. However, to translate the word by such expressions as 'adulterating' or 'doctoring', with their implications of falsification and dishonesty, would be altogether unfair. Indeed, it would be quite wrong to speak of such wines in condescending terms at all. 'Improving' is permitted within limits by law, which lays down not only a maximum amount but also the span of time within which it is allowed. It consists in adding a sugar solution, not to the wine, but to the must during fermentation. The extraneous sugar combines with the grape-sugar, and this, as a unity, is turned into alcohol. In this way a wine can be produced which in alcohol, sugar and acid content more or less equals a natural wine produced from the same site in a better year. It takes an experienced palate to tell an improved wine developed in a good cellar from a natural one. A wine-label does not have to indicate that the wine has been artificially improved; on the other hand, to designate an improved wine as natural is illegal.

The sweetness of a wine may also be increased without the addition of extraneous sugar. As everyone knows, the natural grape-sugar of the must is converted into alcohol through the process of fermentation. However, both natural and artificially sweetened wines may contain a certain proportion of remaining unfermented sugar. They may, or may not, be 'durchgegoren', meaning fermented right through, a very important difference. In the case of a top-grade wine the natural sugar content is so high that it cannot ferment into alcohol without leaving a considerable amount of residual sugar anyway, as the yeast producing fermentation stops acting when a certain level of alcohol has been reached. In this case, the process of fermentation is terminated naturally; the wine is fermented right through and still retains a high degree of natural sugar. On the other hand, the cellar-master may have in his vats a still-fermenting must promising a wine with a good natural-sugar content and corresponding moderate acidity; he may consider that if fermentation were to go through he would get a wine of high alcoholic content but a little deficient in sweetness, whereas if fermentation could be stopped he would get a sweeter yet still sufficiently alcoholic wine. If he interrupts fermentation before it stops by itself he artificially interferes with a natural process; the wine is not fermented right through, and purists might object.

Another method of artificial interference is that of blending one wine with another in order to obtain a more palatable product. The simplest case would be to blend two wines from the same site but of different vintages, for instance, one from a hot and dry year that has an abundant alcoholic and sugar content but insufficient acidity with another from a previous poor year that is somewhat lacking in alcohol and sugar but has plenty of acidity. However, a blend may contain more than two parts, also parts from different localities, even from different regions, as long as all are German wines—only in the case of red wines is the addition of up to twenty-five per cent of foreign products permitted. The name of the blend is determined by that of the locality which has contributed at least two-thirds of the total, thus leaving its predominant stamp on the general character of the product. A blend may be described as a natural wine if none of its parts have been artificially sugared; it may even be described as a 'Spätlese' or 'Auslese' (see below, p. 35f), provided that all of its parts have a claim to these quality designations. Also wines from different grapes may be blended, for example, a Gewürztraminer, whose bouquet is often found too obtrusive and in need of toning down, may be blended with a Riesling or White Burgundy of equal quality.

What is absolutely anathema is the addition of pure alcohol in any quantity at all.

The statements of a wine-label are prescribed by law. They have to indicate (1) the wine-growing region, (2) the vintage year, (3) the name of the locality of origin, (4) the name of the site within the boundaries of the locality, and (5) the kind of grape (e.g., Riesling, Silvaner, etc.). The last condition is not always observed, for example, in a region predominantly producing Silvaner the name may not appear on the label because it is generally taken for granted that, unless it is specifically designated otherwise, the bottle can only contain Silvaner wine. The law does not require a producer to indicate that his wine is natural if it has not been treated artificially by sugaring, but obviously it is in every producer's interest to do so. Consequently, every wine that can be proved to be natural will be characterized by the addition 'Natur' or 'naturrein' (naturally pure). The words 'Wachstum' or 'Kreszenz' (growth), followed by the name of the producer, indicate that the grapes come exclusively from one property and imply that the wine is naturally pure. The designation 'Originalabfüllung' indicates that the wine has been developed and bottled in the cellar of an individual producer, or of a state-owned estate, or of a growers' co-operative; this again guarantees that it is naturally pure.

To the surprise of many, the term 'Natur' or 'naturrein', hitherto an absolute corner-stone of viticultural nomenclature, is to disappear from designations in accordance with the new German wine-law, which was effective from July, 1971. So are the designations 'Wachstum', 'Kreszenz', 'Originalabfüllung', and a few more (see below, p. 74ff). What remains are the following 'predicates', or quality designations, all of which are exclusively reserved for naturally pure wines. They begin at the bottom with 'Cabinet' (or 'Kabinett'), and rise via 'Spätlese', 'Auslese', 'Beerenauslese' to the pinnacle of 'Trockenbeerenauslese'. The special quality of a Spätlese or Auslese may also be emphasized by the adjectives 'feine' or 'feinste' (fine, finest), but only up to and including the 1970 vintage; as from 1971, they are also banned by the new wine law.

The designation 'Cabinet' has spread from the Rheingau, but is not represented everywhere, not in the Moselle region, for example, nor in Baden and Württemberg. Historically it goes back to a cellar of the Eberbach monastery dubbed the 'Cabinet cellar'. This name came officially into being, in 1812, by decree of the Duke of Nassau, who after the secularization had become the lucky heir of the Cistercian monks. They had not known the word. It denoted the venue of the duke's cabinet meetings, and at the same time the depository of his best wine for his own and his ministers' refreshment during consultations. But also Johannisberg claims a historical right to the title 'Cabinet wine', an even older one, though it does not have a cellar known as a 'Cabinet cellar'. This claim is based on the fact that during the eighteenth century its best wines went into a separate cellar in the palace of the Prince Abbot, later Prince Bishop, of Fulda. The contents of this cellar were under a strictly separate administration, known as the 'Secret Cabinet', hence these wines came to be known as 'Cabinet wines', a name that was later continued after Prince Metternich had become the master of Johannisberg Castle. Both Eberbach and Johannisberg may share a rueful feeling that a designation which once stood for the perfection of their wines should now have been demoted to the bottom of the 'predicate' list. But then they missed securing copyright for it in the first place. Or was there no such thing at the time?

The word 'Spätlese' means late gathering; it may be applied only to natural wines made from fully-ripened grapes gathered after the closure of the official harvesting period. As has been explained before, the beginning of the harvesting period is decided officially and is binding on all growers. But every grower is free to gamble on the weather, leaving at least some of his grapes on the vines for further ripening and picking them a shorter or longer while after the end of the general harvest. 'Auslese' means a gathering of selected grapes, characterizing wines produced exclusively from carefully selected fully ripe or over-ripe grapes after eliminating all unripe, damaged or diseased ones. 'Beeren-auslese' goes a step further in demanding a stricter standard of selection: that is, over-ripe berries picked individually from especially favoured sites and covered with 'Edelfäule', that is, 'noble mould' or 'noble rot' (French: *noble pourriture*). This expression designates the beneficial action of a fungus, *Botrytis cinerea*, on fully ripened grapes; it covers the grape with a grey coating, rotting the skin, extracting watery and acid content and concentrating juice and sugar. The highest quality is indicated by the term 'Trockenbeerenauslese', or selection of dry berries; this means the individual picking of over-ripe grapes which, in addi-tion to being daubed with noble mould, have shrunk on the vine to a raisin-like condition.

The two highest degrees of quality are attainable, however, only under the very best weather conditions. They require a warm and dry late summer and early autumn, and a warm but more humid October, the humidity caused by the morning mists which characterize that month. Again, these October mists should not arrive too early, so that the *Botrytis* mould settles on fully ripened grapes. If it settles on unripe ones, for instance in a wet September, it is not noble and beneficial at all but very destructive. But even supposing that, in ideal weather conditions, it has done its work really nobly, it is obvious that any increase in quality can only be achieved at the expense of quantity. It is possible, though rare, to buy a bottle of Auslese in the cellar of a grower's co-operative. It is only the large producer who can afford to go in for any

quantities of Beerenauslese or Trockenbeerenauslese; and in spite
of the high prices that these wines fetch, he does it not for
business reasons but for reasons of prestige. And, another fly in
the ointment, the mould of the *Botrytis cinerea* can be beneficial,
under the favourable conditions mentioned, only to white-wine
grapes; if it befalls red-wine grapes it destroys the pigment and is
absolutely ruinous.

The chance discovery of the beneficial effect of noble mould
and generally the practice of late gathering is connected with a
story of a remarkable vintage at Johannisberg in the late eighteenth
century. Up to that time, the prospect of grapes beginning to rot
on the vine was greatly feared; consequently it was general practice to complete harvesting by mid-October. As has been said
before, the local monastery was at the time under the jurisdiction
of the Benedictine Abbey at Fulda, which is nearly a hundred
miles away as the crow flies. So a mounted courier carrying
a sample of grapes had to be sent every autumn to obtain
the superior prelate's official permission to begin the picking.
However, on one occasion the courier, for some reason or other,
did not return in time. The Johannisberg monks, seeing their
grapes getting mouldier and mouldier, became more and more
dispirited, and by the time the courier at last arrived back with
the official permission everybody expected a miserable vintage.
All the more were they surprised when it turned out the best
ever in living memory. This story has long been relegated to the
folklore category, but its essential historicity, including the fact
that it refers to the year 1775, has since been confirmed by documentary evidence. Only the length and especially the cause of the
courier's delay cannot be verified, and explanatory tales are still
being told with variable embellishments.

There is another high-quality wine which does not figure in
this scale of eminence, because it owes its quality to different
natural conditions. It is 'Eiswein' (Ice-wine), a rarity not produced
by every vintage. The story goes that at one grape-harvest in the
1880s the picking had to be interrupted owing to a sudden break
of frost, and that the growers feared that the as yet unpicked

grapes would be spoiled. Much to their surprise, they found that the wine produced from the frozen grapes was excellent. As a result of the frost, the berries had lost some of their juice but greatly increased their must gravity. Occasionally ice-wines may also result when in late autumn rain is suddenly followed by frost, so that the fully-ripened grapes are coated with a very thin film of ice causing a concentration of their content.

In addition to the ordinary label, bottles may also have special seals attesting the quality of the wine. They are awarded by an official neutral board of examiners, who test the wines as to whether they correspond to the strictures of the German winelaw, whether they represent the special character of their region of origin, whether they are faultless in colour, clearness and taste, etc. The quality seal for which producers of any German wine can apply is the 'Deutsches Weinsiegel' (German Wine Seal). It does not exclude 'improved' wines as long as they conform to the general conditions. There are further regional quality seals which are more exacting in their conditions, for instance, in demanding a really above-average quality and in excluding 'improved' wines. An example is the 'Gütezeichen' (Quality sign) awarded by the Baden Wine-growers' Association. However, while such seals are certainly meant to, and generally do, protect the purchaser, one may find that state domains, large private producers and even growers' co-operatives producing excellent wines, apparently do not bother to apply for such awards. They seem to think, often quite rightly, that their products have no need for any additional paper ornaments stuck on the bottles.

5. Vinification and storing

THIS TERM, vinification, denotes the conversion of grape-juice
into alcoholic wine by fermentation. It is a comprehensive term
which includes the whole of the cellar treatment from the delivery
of the grapes to the storage of the bottled wine. It does not seem
to be used in Germany, where its usual equivalent is 'Keller-
wirtschaft' (cellar management). Some of the cellar processes,
such as improving, blending, stopping of fermentation, mash-
fermentation of red-wine grapes, have already been mentioned.
The technology of the cellar-work is an applied science in its own
right, and can here only be touched upon in the broadest outlines.[9]
The traditional huge and often picturesque wooden winepresses,
which were worked by manual labour, have been museum pieces
for a long time. They are now generally replaced by mechanical
presses of various systems and designs, mostly horizontally placed
cylindrical devices of stainless steel. On the other hand, the oaken
wine-casks, used both for fermentation and for storage, in larger
and smaller sizes to hold different units of quantity, slightly varying in shape from one region to another and often beautifully
carved, are still very much in evidence. In large cellarage works
with their multifarious gadgetry, huge cylindrical glass-lined
metal tanks with a much higher capacity as well as rectangular
concrete containers are the dominant features of the scenery (Plate
11). Fermentation cellar, storage cellar and bottle-cellar are always
separate.

Normal fermentation may begin already a day or two after

pressing and come to an end within a week or little more. The emerging young wine, still muddy with yeast and fizzy with carbonic acid, is a popular beverage in many parts and known as 'Federweisser' (feather-white) or by some other local name. Fermentation in steel pressure tanks, which may take up to four weeks or more, is referred to as 'gezügelte Gärung' (restrained fermentation). Some time after fermentation has ceased, the young wine is racked off, that is, drawn from the yeasty lees by transferring it to another cask. The time chosen for this operation has something to do with the degree of acidity contained in the wine: where it is low, the racking may take place already in late November or early December; where it is high it usually takes place in January or even later. A second racking may be necessary when after the first the young wine has not sufficiently clarified; it is usually done eight or more weeks later and combined with filtration and a chemical treatment known as blue-fining. In special circumstances there may be even further rackings. In all this treatment there is a good deal of variability. Generally speaking, a normal healthy wine develops best the more it is left in peace.

When the wine is left to itself in the storage cask or tank natural changes take place within it, the sum of which is usually called its 'Ausbau', meaning its maturing or gradual development to an optimal condition. How long a wine is left in the storage cask depends on a series of factors. Generally speaking, wines are bottled much earlier nowadays than they were in the past, when they used to be kept in the cask for years. Compared with a metal tank, a wooden cask is of course not absolutely air-tight, and in a long cask storage the wine is always to some extent exposed to damaging influences. Table-wines may be kept in the cask or tank for half a year or a little more; quality wines for about a year; the more valuable ones, including Late Burgundy red wines, which are late also in maturing, for two years. The tail-end of maturation takes place in the bottle. Good Rieslings, Traminers, Ruländers, or Late Burgundies require two to three years of bottle storage to reach full maturity.

Tasting, Buying, Storing

The following remarks do not necessarily apply to German wines only. Similar suggestions will be found, in some form or other, in most popular wine-books. The more sophisticated amateur will skip them; to learner-amateurs they may be useful.

TASTING: In sampling wines, one does not wish to impair one's senses of smell and taste. Some self-evident *Don'ts* are: to avoid any hot food before the tasting; not to smoke during the tasting nor, preferably, immediately before; and, as for ladies, not to use any strong perfumes. Also, not to eat during the tasting, except in between, a mouthful of dry white bread to clear one's palate for the next wine. One samples the bouquet with short sniffs while gently swirling the wine in the glass. In books and pamphlets, the learner-taster may find the Latin tag 'Colore, Odore, Sapore' (mostly also shortened to the COS rule), meaning that wines should be judged by colour, fragrance, and taste, in that sequence. Another often-repeated maxim as to sequence, is to taste the lighter before the stronger wine, the drier before the sweeter, the dry white wine before the red wine, and the red one before the sweet white one.

WHERE TO BUY WINES: From the specialist of course, either the reputable wine-trade or the producer. It has been the writer's practice to sample and buy his supplies from producers whom he has come to know well over the years, from state domains, from owners or managers of larger estates, or from the cellars of growers' co-operatives, and have them shipped to this country. An additional pleasure of the direct method is that of continued new exploration from one year to the next.

TEMPERATURE AND STORING: Temperature should be treated delicately. White wine should come upon the table at between 10° and 12° centigrade; red wine should have room temperature, about 16° to 18° centigrade. To keep bottles of white wine for hours or even days in the refrigerator is rank barbarism; if served too cold the wine loses its fragrance and bouquet on the tongue. Half an hour or a little more in the refrigerator may be permissible if the storage temperature is too high. It may be too low for red wines. They should on no account be brought up to room temperature too suddenly, for instance, by putting the bottles in hot water, in front of an open fire, or too near central-heating radiators. They should be placed in the room several hours before being opened.

The ideal storage room is of course a proper cool wine-cellar, at any rate for white wine. If that is not available, bottles should be kept in the coolest place in the house, and well away from perishable victuals. Experts seem to be at variance about the proper storage place for red wines; some prefer to store them cool together with the white ones, others advocate a separate storage place with ordinary room temperature. But, whether white or red, bottles should not be kept standing up but lying in bins, so that the bottom end of the cork is immersed in and kept moist by the liquid.

6. The German Wine-growing Regions

No INTRODUCTION to the wines of a country would be complete without a description of its wine-growing regions. Chiefly for reasons of space, the following characterization of the German regions can only be rather cursory, selective and therefore uneven.[10]

However, before embarking on a Cooks' Tour of the German winelands, it may be useful to point out some inconsistencies in the regional allocation of wines. These go back partly to the post-war political reorganization of the Federal Republic, partly to territorial changes which took place during the nineteenth century, partly even to medieval history. At present, four Länder, or states, include ten wine-growing regions, *viz.*, Rhineland-Palatinate (Ahr, Moselle with its tributaries Saar and Ruwer, Nahe, Middle Rhine, Rhine-Hesse and Palatinate), Hesse (Rheingau), Baden-Württemberg (Baden and Württemberg), and Bavaria (Franconia). Saar wines do not belong to the Saarland state because they grow along the lower course of the river in Rhineland-Palatinate. Rhine-Hesse wines do not belong to Hesse because their homeland has been detached from the old Hesse and included in the new Rhineland-Palatinate. Prior to the post-war reorganization, Palatinate wines were a Bavarian product, because their homeland was then an outlying part of that state. In its north-western corner, the river Nahe forms for a short stretch the boundary of the Palatinate, and there are two tributaries of the river coming from the Palatinate. The wines grown there are sometimes claimed to be Palatinate wines—and presumably they are for statistical purposes—, though in character they are clearly Nahe wines.

Rheingau wines belong to the reconstituted state of Hesse. The easternmost wine-growing community of that region, Hochheim, does not belong to the Rheingau geographically, being situated to the north of the lower Main near its junction with the Rhine, yet its wine is sufficiently similar to those of the Rheingau proper to qualify for inclusion in that category. However, geography and political co-ordination, or rather geography and history, come into conflict beyond the bend of the Rhine between Rüdesheim and Assmannshausen, the stretch often named 'Lower Rheingau'. Assmannshausen, which specializes in red wine, may be conceded special status; but to classify the products of Lorch and Lorchhausen farther down as Rheingau wines is a little odd. They are geographically and consequently in character wines of the Middle Rhine, as are those of Kaub a few miles down the river or of Bacharach on the other side of it. The basic reason for their inclusion in the Rheingau category is the historical fact that for many centuries before the secularization of 1803 the frontier of 'Kurmainz', the ecclesiastical electorate of Mainz, which also included the whole of the Rheingau proper, ran between Lorchhausen and Kaub. This historical frontier, and with it the triumph of history over geography, has again been confirmed in the postwar political reorganization of 1945: Lorchhausen is still included in the state of Hesse, whereas Kaub belongs to Rhineland-Palatinate, which makes its wine officially Middle Rhine.

Another oddity is the artificial distinction between two kinds of Bergstrasse wines. This region is the stretch of country between Darmstadt and Heidelberg, hugging the foothills of the Odenwald. It is a geographical unit, and its wines are more or less of the same kind. Sometimes it is indeed quite rightly acknowledged as a separate region, in which case not ten but eleven regions are recognized. But more often political claims interfere with geographical reality. The Bergstrasse has the bad fortune that at about half-way along its length it is crossed by the border between the states of Hesse and Baden-Württemberg, which makes the wines of the northern half Hesse wines, an appendage of those of the Rheingau, and those of the southern half Baden wines, thus reducing the number of regions to ten.

The pre-war states of Baden and Württemberg, both owing their frontiers to Napoleon, have retained their respective territories, but have been politically merged into the new state of Baden-Württemberg. Yet their respective wine-regions have not been merged. Each of the two is extremely jealous of the separate identity of its wines. At the same time, there can be no greater local diversity than between different wines included in the category of Baden wines. The country is not a single wine-growing region but an agglomerate of regions. Although for the greater part Baden is separated from Württemberg by the Black Forest, nevertheless in the north, where the Neckar crosses over from Württemberg into Baden, there is hardly any difference in the wines grown along adjoining stretches of the river. And again, in the extreme north-east of the country, where the Tauber valley joins that of the Main, the character of the Tauber wines of Baden blends with that of the Franconian wines of Bavaria.

The simplest sequence in which to describe the regions would be that according to the size of their production.[11] This puts the Palatinate, in German Pfalz or Rheinpfalz, which produces a quarter or more of the German total, in the first place. The name is derived from a term applied to a semi-autonomous territory in the medieval German state, which was ruled by a Comes Palatinus, Count Palatine, or Pfalzgraf. But before this title became that of a territorial ruler it was, in the Frankish kingdom, that of a high palace official. And this, again, links up with the ancient Roman tradition: Augustus had his residence on the Palatium, one of the seven hills of Rome, and ever since the word palatium came to mean the imperial residence, or palace, and palatinus a dignitary belonging to it.

However, to come back to our region, the Palatinate is roughly divided into two halves, western and eastern, by a wooded hill-range named the Pfälzerwald or the Hardt (also spelt Haardt or

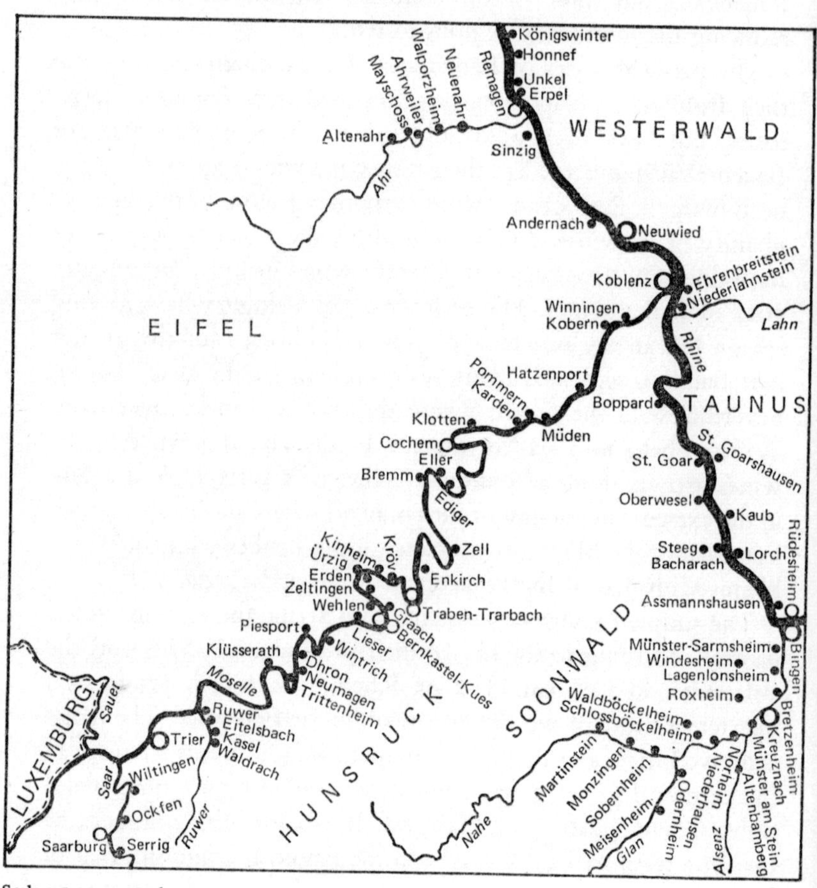

Scale : 1 cm = 10·5 km

Hart). The wine-growing localities, some of them smallish towns, others small villages, are strung out along the 'Weinstrasse', which runs from the border of Alsace to that of Rhine-Hesse at a length of 50 miles, hugging the foothills of the Hardt. The vineyard belt has an average width of three miles, and a good deal of it is on flat ground; it is protected from the western winds by the Hardt. Eastwards, the Weinstrasse does not come anywhere in sight of the Rhine, which runs about 15 miles to the east of it between entirely flat banks. But any geographical disadvantages are offset by the climate of the region, which is reputed to be the warmest in Germany (though it may be outmatched by that of the Kaiserstuhl in southern Baden). At any rate, the Palatinate Weinstrasse is a stretch of country where almonds and sweet chestnuts, figs and mulberries, peaches and apricots flourish and ripen. There is considerable variability in the composition of the soil, with variegated sandstone, loess and loam, marl and limestone predominating.

Geographically the Weinstrasse is divided, from south to north, into the Oberhardt, Mittelhardt and Unterhardt. The Upper Hardt produces predominantly, and in considerable quantities, Silvaner wines of mild and modest quality. Also the Lower Hardt goes in mainly for Silvaner, which here, however, grows chiefly on heavy limestone soil and is on the whole milder and softer than that of the Upper Hardt. It is the Middle Hardt which is mainly responsible for the great reputation of Palatinate wines. This section begins at Neustadt an der Weinstrasse, the centre of the local wine trade and seat of a research and teaching college. Rieslings make up only fourteen per cent of the total Palatinate production; they come virtually all from the Middle Hardt. Two neighbouring communities, Deidesheim and Forst, the latter a tiny village, rival for recognition as top places. Deidesheim, situated largely on volcanic rock, is famous for its sites Grain, Kieselberg, Hahnenböhl, Rennpfad, Klostergarten, Kalkofen, Langenmorgen, Herrgottsacker, and others. At Forst the visitor will be assured that the local soil has the greatest 'Bonität' (a rather old-fashioned loan-word from the French bonté), and no wonder since the place sits on a patch of basalt. Its great sites are Jesuiten-garten, Ungeheuer, Margaretenbrunnen, Mariengarten, Lange-nacker, Hellholz, Kranich, Elster, Schnepfenflug, and others. Nearby are Ruppertsberg with its sites Goldschmied, Nussbien, Reiterpfad, etc.; Wachenheim with its Gerümpel, Fuchsmantel, Goldbächel, Schenkenböhl, etc.; Dürkheim, a spa, with another Schenkenböhl, a Hochbenn, Nonnengarten, Spielberg, etc.; Ung-stein with its Honigsäckel; Kallstadt with its Saumagen, etc., etc. The Rieslings of the better Middle Hardt sites are more full-bodied and fiery, richer in bouquet than those of most other regions. Also Traminers and Muscatels are grown, and of course also Silvaners which are fuller and stronger here than in the Upper and Lower Hardt. Lastly, there is the Palatinate red wine, mostly from Dürkheim and the bulk of it coming from the humble Portugieser vine.

Rhine-Hesse (Rheinhessen), to the north of the Palatinate and less than a quarter of its size, is the second-largest producer. It is a country of low, gently rolling hill-ranges, approximately tri-angular in shape between the three riverside cities of Worms, Mainz and Bingen. Viticulturally it may be divided, very roughly, into five sub-regions: the Bingen area extending a short distance along the lower Nahe river; the Ingelheim area between Bingen and Mainz; the Rhine front extending from some distance south of Mainz to some distance north of Worms; the Worms area, sometimes called the 'Wonnegau'; and the valley and general neighbourhood of the river Selz which runs northwards from Alzey to join the Rhine near Ingelheim.

In the neighbourhood of Worms—e.g., near Osthofen and Westhofen, and along the string of villages here included under the term 'Rhine front': Mettenheim, Alsheim, Guntersblum, Ludwigshöhe, Dienheim, as far as the town of Oppenheim, and again farther north at Bodenheim and Laubenheim—the vines stand mostly on loess and clayey soils. The gently sloping vine-yards of these places are not far from the Rhine, but not near enough to reap the benefit which the broad expanse of water bestows on the grapes. This is the case only in the relatively short

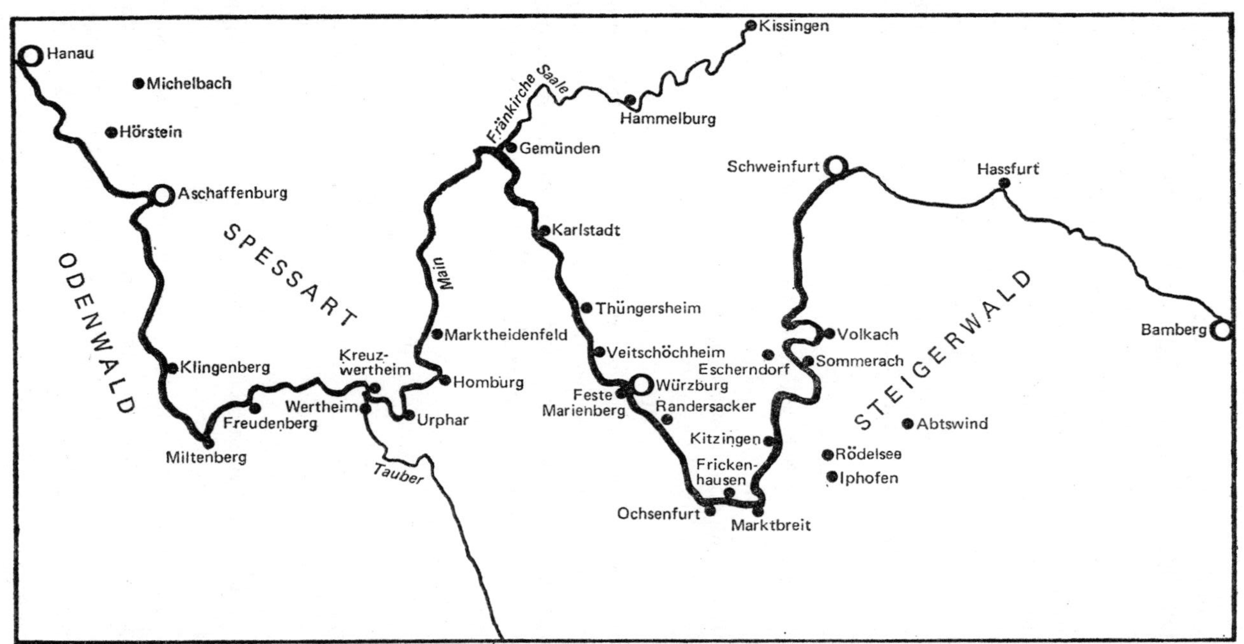

Scale : 1 cm = 9.5 km

intervening section of the Rhine front, from Oppenheim to Nierstein and Nackenheim, and especially between the two last-named places. Here the hill-range bearing the vineyards becomes much higher and steeper and immediately approaches the river. And there is also a change of soil. This soil is often mistaken for red sandstone, but is in fact red argillaceous slate, often called in German 'Rotliegendes' (red-lier). It crumbles into flat pebbles, producing a terrible scree on the steep slopes. Nor is it really red but more of a dark purplish colour; but when, in heavy downpours, some of it is washed down into the Rhine, it paints the water crimson for many miles. This soil is especially rich in nutritive substance for the vines. In the centre of the country, the environment of the Selz valley, clayey and somewhat impermeable soils predominate; the Bingen area has predominantly slate soils; that of Ingelheim loose sandy soils.

In quantity of production, the Silvaner vine preponderates; its proportion is higher than in the Palatinate, while that of the Riesling vine is substantially lower than in the Palatinate. Ingelheim specializes in red wines of the Early and Late Burgundy varieties. The Rieslings are chiefly grown on the Rhine front stretch between Oppenheim and Nackenheim, and especially on the steeply inclined 'red-lier' sites between Nierstein and Nackenheim, which immediately face the river and benefit from the reflection of light and warmth. In the larger local estates, Rieslings amount to seventy per cent of the total production. They are distinguished by a remarkably great body, roundness and bouquet. It is on them that the high reputation of Rhine-Hesse wines is chiefly founded. But also Silvaners attain their very best quality on this short stretch of the Rhine front. Again, the steeply sloping sites of Bingen produce some quite outstanding Rieslings.

Lastly, some site names from these most favoured parts. Oppenheim: Sackträger, Reisekahr, Herrnberg, Goldberg, Zuckerberg, Schlossberg, Kreuz, Guldenmorgen, etc. The most widely known local name, Krötenbrunnen, is not a site name but a so-called 'Gattungsname' (generic name), which may be used for any wine grown within a half-radius of 15 kilometres. Nierstein: Glöck,

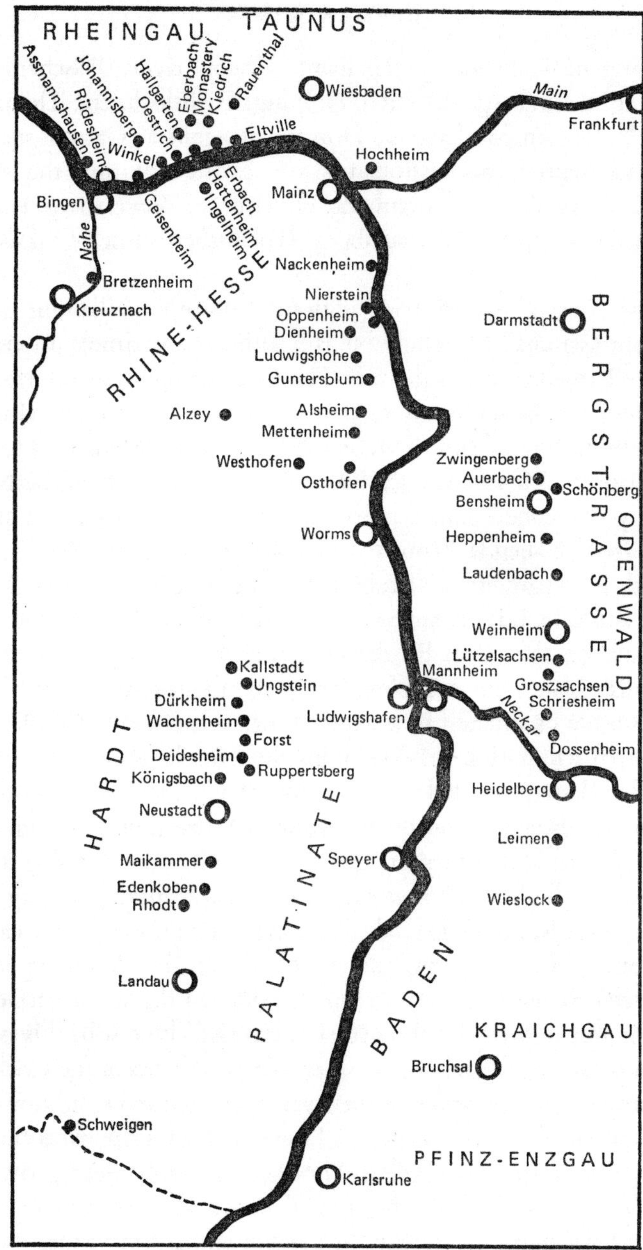

Scale : 1 cm = 8·5 km

Auflangen, Rehbach, Spiegelberg, Orbel, Kehr, Fläschenhahl, Ölberg, Kranzberg, Pettental, Hipping, Fuchsloch, etc. The most widely known local name, Domtal, is again a 'Gattungsname' (generic name), permissible for any product within the same range. Nackenheim: Rotenberg, Engelsberg, Weyersberg, Kirchberg, etc. Bingen: Scharlachberg, Rochusberg, Eisel, Ohlisberg, etc.

The Moselle-Saar-Ruwer region. 'Vinum mosellanum omni tempore sanum' (Moselle wine is healthy at any time): no visitor to the Moselle escapes the tag. The German name of the river is Mosel, with the accent on the first syllable; the Latin form Mosella is a diminutive of Mosa, the name of the river Meuse; so to the Romans the Moselle was the little Meuse. The river flows between deeply-embedded banks, most of its way meandering in a series of narrow U-bends. From the Luxemburg border to Koblenz its length is 125 miles; the straight distance is only 75 miles. On its northern side, it is protected from cold winds and rain by the Eifel plateau, on the south by the Hunsrück range, both part of the Rhenish Slate Hills complex. Trier, the main centre of the local wine-trade, is situated in a wider, more open valley. Of the two southern tributaries, the Saar joins the Moselle above, the much smaller Ruwer just below Trier. Wherever there is an exposure to the south, according to the change of direction sometimes on the left and sometimes on the right bank, the steep slopes are planted with vines. The sunlight is reflected from the river against the vineyards; this beneficial effect has been increased by the canalization of the river since the 1950s, which, by damming it up between eleven locks, has greatly broadened the water surface.

The upper Moselle, above Trier, has shell-lime soil; this is the main refuge of the Elbling vine, which also recurs in the Cochem 'Krampen', a large bulge of the river where natural conditions are not suitable for better varieties. Elsewhere, with the exception of a limited amount of Müller-Thurgau, the only vine grown is Riesling. It stands throughout on slate soil which has the advantage of warming up quickly in the sun and storing much of the warmth during the night. But there is a difference between the slate of the middle Moselle, including Saar and Ruwer, and that of the lower Moselle. The former stretches have a bluish-grey argillaceous slate which crumbles easily into a nutritive, moisture-retaining soil. The slate of the lower course of the river is interspersed with iron, reddish-grey in colour, hard and weathering only insufficiently; thus it is poor in nutritive substance and moisture-retaining capacity. Another disadvantage of the lower Moselle, below Cochem, is that the river assumes a much straighter north-eastern course where slopes with a southern aspect become rare. The Moselle, and especially its lower course, has the steepest vineyard slopes of Germany; almost incredibly steep, with an overall gradient of 65°, is the large Calmont site between Eller and Bremm.

It is often felt that the whole atmosphere of the Moselle valley 'breathes slate'. Also local names refer to slate, namely, the word 'Lay', here still understood as denoting slate, though obsolete elsewhere in Germany. It occurs, by itself, occasionally as the name of a village or of a site, but there are hundreds of site names in which it forms part of a compound: Rotlay, Schwarzlay, Urlay, Kranklay, Günterslay, Hubertuslay, Eulenlay, Busslay, Herzlay, Klosterlay, Münzlay, Geierslay, Burglay, etc.

Moselle Rieslings are on the whole lighter, somewhat less alcoholic, also less full-bodied, but more airy and fragrant than those of other regions. They mostly have a very pleasant fruity acidity. Those of the Saar especially are remarkable for their naturally sparkling and prickly quality. All Rieslings of the Moselle region have a basic individuality of their own, which makes it relatively easy to distinguish them from those of other regions. However, partly owing to the many undulations in the course of the river, and partly to differences in the subsoil below the slate, the natural conditions of different sites vary of course a great deal, and this accounts for a considerable variability in the flavour and taste of different local wines.

There are 180 wine-growing communities in the Moselle region, and any mention of names cannot avoid arbitrariness. The middle Moselle holds names of high distinction: Clüsserath with its widely-known site Bruderschaft, etc.; Trittenheim with its equally well-known Altärchen, Apotheke, etc.; Piesport with its still better-known Goldtröpfchen, etc., and Brauneberg with its Juffer. Then we come to the little town of Bernkastel with its famous Doctor, a wine which has earned its name by reputedly having saved the life of a medieval archbishop, and which in the first decade of this century had its lustre refurbished when King Edward VII had it prescribed for the good of his liver by his physician in ordinary. Other local sites are Badstube, Lay, Johannisbrünnchen, etc. Here the Moselle takes a turn to the north-west, but the vineyards on its right bank face more south than south-west. The village of Graach specializes in theological and ecclesiastical names: Himmelreich, Petrus, Kirchlay, Abtsberg, Domprobst, Bistum, etc. Wehlen follows with its famous Sonnenuhr, etc., Zeltingen with another Himmelreich, etc. At the next turn of the river we come to Ürzig with its well-known Würzgarten, etc.; Erden with Treppchen, Busslay, etc.; Kienheim with Hubertuslay, etc.; Kröv with its somewhat coarsely named Nacktarsch (not a site-name), etc.; the twin-town of Traben-Trarbach with Geierslay, another Würzgarten, etc.; Enkirch with Herrenberg, etc. On the lower Saar river, Wiltingen, Ockfen, Saarburg and Serrig are the best-known wine-growing communities; on the Ruwer, Eitelsbach, Mertesdorf, Kasel and Waldrach.

Baden is characterized by a relative rareness of larger estates, the predominance of small vineyard holdings between half an acre and two acres, mostly worked by mixed farmers, and a corresponding density of growers' co-operatives. Of the larger estates, probably the biggest are run by the state, e.g. the Meersburg domain on Lake Constance with about a hundred acres and that of the Blankenhornsberg in the Kaiserstuhl area with about fifty acres; those in private, especially aristocratic, ownership are mostly confined to the Ortenau area of central Baden. Baden has a greater diversity in the composition of soils and in climate than other regions, and consequently, in marked contrast especially to Moselle wines, those of Baden have no unity of character. As has

Plate 9 (above). Johannisberg Castle in the Rheingau.
Photo by courtesy of the Manager.

Plate 9 (below). View of the Pfälzerwald range, vineyards of the
Middle Hardt and the Rhine plain, Palatinate.
Photo by courtesy of Deutsche Wein-Information, Mainz.

Plate 10 (above). Wine-cellar of Johannisberg Castle, the vault completely covered
by Kellertuch (cellar-cloth, the fungus Cladisporium cellare).

Photo by courtesy of Deutsche Wein-Information.

Plate 10 (below). Cellar with traditional, now obsolete, wooden
wine-presses and vats, Eberbach Monastery.

Photo by courtesy of the Director, Hesse State Domains.

Plate 11. Modern metal fermentation tanks, Central Cellarage of the
Baden Wine-growers' Co-operatives, Breisach.

Photo by courtesy of the Manager.

Plate 12 (above). Spätlese (Late Gathering) of Ruländer grapes in a Kaiserstuhl vineyard.

Plate 12 (below). Expert tasters of Baden wines.

Photo by courtesy of the Manager, Central Cellarage, Breisach.

Plate 13 (above). From left (1) 1964 Kaiserstuhl Ruländer Auslese, from Leiselheim (village) Gestühl (site); the top label saying that it was awarded the Great Prize of the Baden Wine-growers' Association, 1967. (2) 1967 Palatinate Traminer Spätlese, from Forst (village) Hellholz (site); Eugen Müller Wine-estate—Wine-cellarage. (3) 1964 Moselle (Riesling) Auslese, from Klüsserath (town) Bruderschaft (site); Wilhelm Faust Cellarage, Traben-Trarbach. (4) 1966 Moselle (Riesling) Spätlese, from Erden (village) Busslay (site); same cellarage. (5) 1967 Rhine-Hesse Sylvaner Spätlese, from Westhofen (village) Liebfrauenberg (site); producer Karl Fr. Groebe, Biebesheim-Westhofen.

Plate 13 (left). Quality sign of Baden Wine-growers' Association.

Plate 14. 1969 Rheingau Riesling Cabinet Spätlese, from Hallgarten (town) Schönhell (site). Original bottling Prince Löwenstein-Wertheim-Rosenberg Wine Estate.

Plate 15 (left). 1964 Moselle (Riesling) Spätlese, from Wehlen (town) Sonnenuhr (site); Growth: Zach. Bergweiler-Prüm Heirs, Wine Estate Dr. Adams-Bergweiler, Bernkastel, Johannishof. Original cellar bottling. (An old wine and the label has suffered from the dampness in the cellar, but this, of course, has no effect upon the contents of the bottle!)

Plate 15 (right). A litre bottle of Müller-Thurgau without indication of vintage year, same origin and producer as Plate 13 top (5). Litre bottles go mainly to taverns and inns and are retailed in Schoopen (¼-litre glasses). Producer's price, DM3—including added value tax of 11 per cent.

Plate 16 (left). 1964 Rheingau Riesling Spätlese from Rauenthal (village) Burggraben (site). Original bottling by the local Wine-growers' Co-operative.
Plate 16 (centre). 1963 Nahe Riesling fine Spätlese from Norheim (village) Kafels (site). Original bottling Wine Estate August Anheuser, Kreuznach Spa.
Plate 16 (right). 1969 (Rhine-Hesse) Riesling Spätlese, from Nackenheim (town) Rotenberg (site); producer (Rhineland-Palatinate) State Wine Domains, Mainz.

been said before, Baden is not a single wine-growing region but rather an agglomerate of separate regions producing wines of different character. Compared with the Palatinate, Rhine-Hesse and some other regions, the percentage of Silvaner is low; it is grown only sporadically.

To begin with Lake Constance (Bodensee), its altitude above sea-level is near the upper limit of vine-cultivation north of the Alps. Another disadvantage would seem to be the kind of the local soil. Vines are adaptable, but here they have to content themselves with a soil that is largely nothing better than moraine till. These handicaps are, however, offset by a very mild climate, a generally southern aspect of vineyard slopes which often extend down to the lake-shore, the reflection of sunlight from a very large sheet of water as well as the effect of the lake in equalizing temperatures. At the present time, only the Meersburg area and the much smaller one of nearby Hagnau remain as producers of any size. In the past, 'Seeweine' (Lake wines) were sometimes considered a bit raw by outsiders, if not by locals, but a substantial improvement has been attained in the last decades, in a large part due to the untiring efforts of the state domain at Meersburg.[12] The wines grown include Müller-Thurgau (Riesling x Silvaner), Ruländer, Traminer, White Burgundy, and Blue Late Burgundy used for red wine as well as for Weissherbst (Rosé), most of them of very respectable quality.

The Markgräflerland, in the foothills of the southern Black Forest between Basle and Freiburg, is especially known for the cultivation of the Gutedel vine, which thrives well in the deep fertile loam soil and the warm and humid climate of the area. Gutedel wines have the advantage of a relative evenness of quality over time; in good and bad years they deviate less from a normal value than do other wines. They are light in alcoholic content, mild, with little acidity, and a gentle bouquet. There are about seventy wine-growing communities in the area. The best-known local and site names are Auggen with its Letten, Müllheim with Reggenhag, Hügelheim with Pflanzer, Britzingen with Sonnhohle, and Laufen with Altenberg.

Situated in the middle of the upper Rhine plain, to the north-west of Freiburg, is an isolated massif of volcanic rock, the Kaiserstuhl. Its climate is hot and dry: the average annual temperature is 10·1°C (as compared with Freiburg's 9·9°C, Trier's 9·2°C and Würzburg's 8·8°C), the average annual rainfall 656 mm (as compared with 869 mm in Freiburg and more between Freiburg and Basle). The loess coat covering the volcanic rock reaches a height of up to seventy feet in places. Until the beginning of the nineteenth century, only Elbling vines were planted on the loess. A change came about 1815, when a physician named Lydtin, a retired army surgeon in Napoleonic service, entered the scene. Inspired by his observation of the cultivation of Lacrimae Christi vines on the slopes of Vesuvius, he started a vineyard on a piece of rocky wasteland, planting it with better varieties of vine. They took root in the black volcanic rock, which retains the heat of the day overnight, and produced a superior wine. The example of this pioneer was followed, in the 1840s, by three brothers named Blankenhorn (one of them the great-grandfather of Herbert Blankenhorn, the previous German ambassador to the United Kingdom), who planted Riesling, Traminer, Ruländer and Late Burgundy vines on the naked rock. The Blankenhornsberg estate near Ihringen, named after them, became a state domain in 1945. Today a considerable proportion of Kaiserstuhl vineyards are on volcanic rock. The most important wine-growing communities are, in the south and south-west, Ihringen, Achkarren, Bickensohl, Bischoffingen, Burkheim, Oberrotweil, Oberbergen and Kiechlinsbergen; in the north, east and south-east, Endingen, Bahlingen, Eichstetten, Bötzingen and Wasen-weiler; the former group is, on the whole, acknowledged as the more favoured one. The Kaiserstuhl produces the most full-bodied and fiery Ruländer found anywhere in Germany, White Burgundy, Silvaner, smaller quantities of Riesling, Traminer and Gewürztraminer, and, for red and Weissherbst (Rosé) wines, Blue Late Burgundy.

The Breisgau area, between Freiburg and the town of Lahr, is not in the same league with the Kaiserstuhl. The prevailing soils are loess, marl and chalky loam, producing a modest country wine for local consumption. There are, of course, exceptions. Freiburg and the Glottertal, a valley to the north of it, have gneiss slopes. The Glottertal produces a very good Blue Late Burgundy, mostly used for the popular 'Weissherbst'. In the immediate environment of Freiburg, the Schlossberg has good Riesling and Traminer and the Lorettoberg equally good Ruländer and Late Burgundy wines.

The Ortenau, situated in the foothills of the Black Forest north of Lahr and as far as Baden-Baden, has fertile soils of crumbling granite and locally also red argillaceous slate ('red-lier'), and very warm and well-protected slopes. Although little-known beyond the frontiers of Baden, local experts speak of this district as the heart of their country's winelands. The kinds of vine grown are Traminer (locally known as Clevner) and Gewürztraminer (the more spicy variety), both more characteristic of the southern Ortenau, the Offenburg area; Ruländer, equally more frequent in the southern part; Riesling (locally known as Klingelberger), more predominant in the northern part, the Bühl area; and Blue Late Burgundy, grown almost anywhere. The Ortenau has its 'Badische Weinstrasse', beginning at Gengenbach in the Kinzig valley and running north-west towards Offenbach, then swinging in and out through most of the wine-growing localities until it reaches Baden-Baden. There is a string of vineyard villages in a half-circle east of Offenbach. A little farther away is Durbach, which has the largest vine-planted surface in the whole of the Ortenau, with a great number of steep slopes facing south on which Traminer, Gewürztraminer, Ruländer and Blue Late Burgundy wines of the highest quality are grown. At Oberkirch and in the vineyards of some villages to the north of it, a certain quantity of Riesling is already planted in addition to the other vines. Waldulm and Kappelrodeck enjoy a high reputation for the quality of their Blue Late Burgundy. In the vineyards of the small towns and villages about Bühl Riesling becomes predominant; but there is one small place, Affental, which bears the palm for the very best Blue Burgundy in the whole of Baden.

On the last stretch, in the vineyards of Steinbach, Neuweier, Varnhalt, Sinzheim and on the Fremersberg slopes near Baden-Baden, Riesling is almost exclusively grown, the 'Mauerwein' of Neuweier being acknowledged to be the best of the Ortenau.

There is little more to be said about the sub-regions of Baden. The Pfinzgau opposite Karlsruhe, the Kraichgau south of Heidelberg and the lower Neckar valley do not produce wines of any great quality. Those of the lower Tauber valley are Franconian wines in character, those of the southern half of the Bergstrasse are not very different from those of the northern half in Hesse. Furthermore, viticulture seems to be more or less on the way out in most parts of northern Baden. It is not as essential here as it is in central and southern Baden, where on steep slopes nothing but the vine can be planted. Also, there are flourishing industries in northern Baden offering easier, safer and more remunerative work than can be found in viticulture.

Like Baden, Württemberg is predominantly a land of small vineyard holdings, many owners being only part-time wine-growers, and a corresponding importance of co-operatives. Natural conditions are on the whole not very favourable to viticulture. Most of the soil is shell–lime and red marl, and as far as climate is concerned, the country is just a little too far east on the map: it is barely sufficient to the north of Stuttgart but increasingly rough south of the city towards the hills of the Rauhe Alp. Württemberg's wines are grown in the winding valleys of the Neckar and its tributaries, especially the Zaber and Enz coming from the west, the Sulm, Murr and Rems from the east. Vineyards are situated, as far as possible, in well protected nooks and crannies of these tortuous valleys. More than half of the production are red wines, most of it from the Trollinger vine, a speciality of Württemberg, producing a pleasantly fresh and pithy wine; smaller quantities from Portugieser, Limberger, Black Riesling and Blue Late Burgundy. There is another Württemberg speciality, namely, the 'Schillerwein', once very popular but now said to become rare. The name is not, as one might believe, a tribute to the poet Friedrich Schiller, Württemberg's great son,

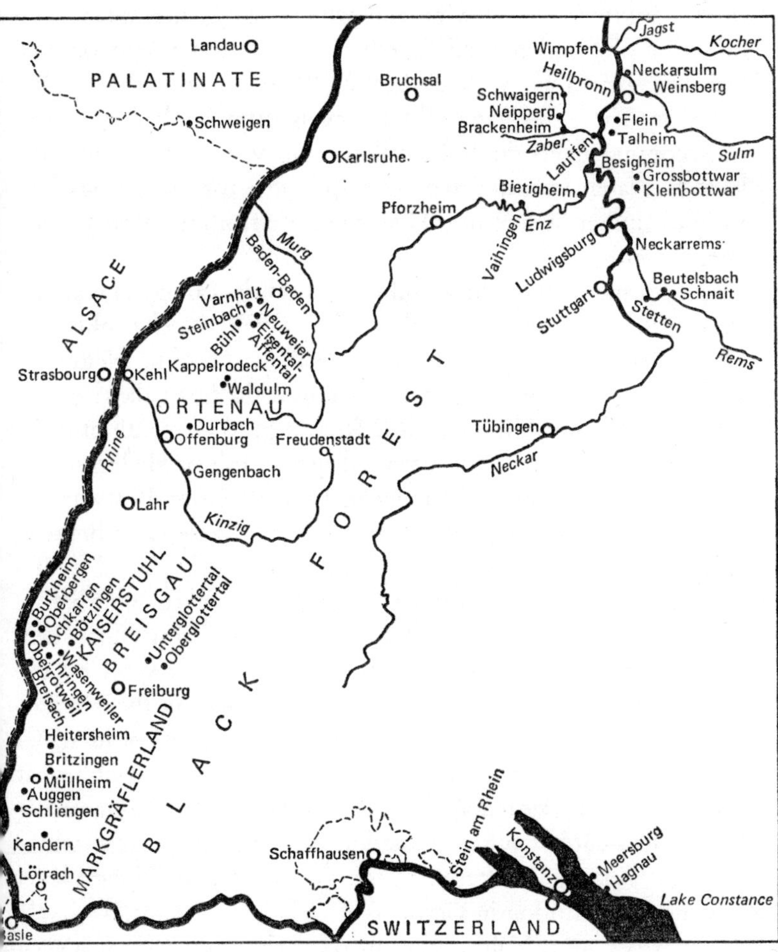

PALATINATE
Landau
Schweigen
ALSACE
Strasbourg
Kehl
Bruchsal
Karlsruhe
Baden-Baden
Varnhalt
Steinbach
Bühl
Neuweier
Eisental
Affental
Kappelrodeck
Waldulm
ORTENAU
Durbach
Offenburg
Gengenbach
Freudenstadt
Murg
Pforzheim
Wimpfen
Jagst
Kocher
Heilbronn
Neckarsulm
Weinsberg
Schwaigern
Neipperg
Brackenheim
Flein
Talheim
Zaber
Lauffen
Sulm
Besigheim
Grossbottwar
Kleinbottwar
Bietigheim
Vaihingen
Enz
Ludwigsburg
Neckarrems
Beutelsbach
Schnait
Stuttgart
Stetten
Rems
BLACK FOREST
Tübingen
Neckar
Rhine
Lahr
Kinzig
Burkheim
Oberbergen
Achkarren
Bötzingen
KAISERSTUHL
BREISGAU
Unterglottertal
Oberglottertal
Oberrotweil
Ihringen
Wasenweiler
Breisach
Freiburg
Heitersheim
Britzingen
Müllheim
Auggen
Schliengen
MARKGRÄFLERLAND
Kandern
Lörrach
Basle
Schaffhausen
Stein am Rhein
Konstanz
Meersburg
Hagnau
Lake Constance
SWITZERLAND
Scale : 1 cm = 16 km

but is taken from the verb 'schillern', meaning to scintillate or to be iridescent. And the reason for this is the fact that it is made from a mixture of red-wine and white-wine grapes planted on the same plot and pressed together. Thus, what might on first sight appear to be a 'Weissherbst' (Rosé) is something quite different. The percentage of Riesling is surprisingly high, most of it coming from the Sulm valley near Weinsberg, where the local Research Institute may be responsible for its propagation, from a number of sites near Heilbronn and from the Rems valley farther south.

Only some of the wine-producing localities can be named. To the north of Heilbronn in the Sulm valley: Neckarsulm and Weinsberg; in and near the Zaber valley: Lauffen, Neipperg, Brackenheim and Schwaigern; in and near the Enz valley: Besigheim, Bietigheim, Vaihingen and Rosswag; to the south of it the Ludwigsburg district with many villages; south of Heilbronn on the eastern side of the Neckar: Flein, Talheim, Gross-Bottwar and Klein-Bottwar; in the Rems valley: Schnait, Stetten and Beutelsbach. No other large city in Germany is so closely ringed with a thick belt of vineyard country as is the Stuttgart conurbation including Cannstatt, Obertürkheim, Untertürkheim and Feuerbach. However, it is slightly outmatched in this respect by the medium-sized town of Heilbronn farther down on the Neckar. Württemberg does not seem to export any quantities of its wines to other parts of Germany, let alone abroad; on the contrary, it is said to import sizeable quantities, especially from neighbouring Baden. Its people have a reputation of being enthusiastic wine-drinkers; indeed, Württemberg is on record for the highest level of wine-consumption in Germany.

The wines of the Nahe region are often characterized—in a very general sense but with some justification—as a kind of blend between Moselle and Rhine wines. The small river comes from the Hunsrück range, runs through a very narrow valley and joins the Rhine just above its bend at Bingen. Its wine-growing region is well protected against north winds by the Soon Wald, an eastern extension of the Hunsrück. In contrast with the Moselle, the soils of the Nahe region are very varied, consisting of loam, red sandstone, red clay, gravelly sand, marl, a good deal of slate, red argillaceous slate ('red-lier'), and above all a good deal of porphyry. These different soils determine the overall diversity and the distinctive local character of Nahe wines. Virtually all of them are white wines, Silvaner, Riesling and Müller-Thurgau being the predominant varieties. On the lower course of the river the wines are generally heavier, more full-bodied and rounded, often with a somewhat earthy taste; higher up more racy, dry, fruity and with a fine bouquet.

Bad Kreuznach, which has a great number of excellent sites in its immediate neighbourhood, is the centre of the local wine-trade, while Niederhausen-Schlossböckelheim, higher up the river, is the seat of the Nahe state domain, with a record of outstanding achievement. The main wine-growing communities situated on the bank of the river are, from Bingen southwards, Münster-Sarmsheim, Laubenheim (no connection with the place of the same name in Rhine-Hesse), Langenlonsheim, Bretzenheim, Kreuznach, Münster am Stein, Norheim, Niederhausen, Schlossböckelheim, and higher up Monzingen and Martinstein, the upper limit. There is a rather greater number of places, some with very impressive wines, situated in lateral valleys more or less far away from the Nahe, e.g., on the left-hand side, Dorsheim and Rümmelsheim in the Trollbach valley; Heddesheim and Windesheim in the Guldenbach valley; Winzenheim north of Kreuznach; Roxheim in the Gräfenbach valley; Weinsheim and Rüdesheim (no connection with the far more important Rheingau town of that name) in the Ellerbach valley; Traisen and Hüffelsheim behind Norheim; Waldböckelheim behind Schlossböckelheim. On the opposite side of the Nahe there are two valleys coming down from the Palatinate hills but producing wines which share the character of the Nahe region, *viz.*, the Alsenz valley with Altenbamberg, Hochstetten, etc., and the Glan valley with Odernheim, Meisenheim, etc.

Only a few names of sites producing good Riesling can be given. Kreuznach: Narrenkappe, Rosengarten, Brückes, Steinweg,

Steinberg, Mönchberg, Kronenberg, Schlossberg, Kahlenberg, Krötenpfuhl, Hinkelstein, St. Martin, etc. Norheim: Kafels, Dellchen, etc. Niederhausen: Hermannshöhle, etc. Schlossböckelheim: Königsberg, Felsenberg, Heimberg, Mühlberg, Kupfergrube, etc.

Rheingau wines have been celebrated by many connoisseurs, including, not unnaturally, some natives of the Rheingau. To quote the judgment of an author who has no ties of local patriotism, the American Frank Schoonmaker writes: 'This seems to be one of those rare corners of the earth that ranks as a sort of vintner's Mother Lode, where sun and soil and one special variety of grape combine with man's help to produce a miracle which cannot be performed or repeated elsewhere.'[13] Indeed, the Rheingau has everything, bar one, to wit, size. Here the Rhine, coming from the south, runs against the barrier of the Taunus range, an eastern extension of the Rhenish Slate Hills complex, and is deflected, for about 18 miles, in a western direction. There is an uninterrupted belt of vineyard slopes, mostly very gently inclined, climbing up from the right bank of the river, virtually all of them with a southern aspect. At their back, the heavily wooded Taunus hills protect them from storms and rain; the north winds, thrown upwards by the heights, clear the sky above the valley but cannot touch the valley itself and its vineyard slopes. The Rhine, on this short stretch, reaches its greatest width, one kilometre across. The broad water surface reflects the sunlight, equalizes the temperature by returning the warmth of the day overnight, and increases the moisture of the air by evaporation, offsetting the dearth of ground moisture in an area of very low rainfall. In the autumn the Rheingau gets heavy mists which favour the development of the 'noble mould'. In conjunction with a favourable climate, there is a favourable composition of soils. It is predominantly deep fertile loam and loess soil shot through with slate and quartzite and covering, at the bottom level, marl and alluvial soils, at any rate a mixture which varies in almost every site and determines a wide range in the taste and flavour ingredients of local Riesling wines, the predominant Rheingau variety.

There are several privately owned large estates, mostly in aristocratic ownership and including those of the castles, e.g., Schloss Reinhartshausen, Schloss Vollrads, Schloss Johannisberg, etc. There are further, dispersed over the whole Rheingau, seven large model domains run by the Administration of the Hesse Vineyard Estates at Eltville: Assmannshausen, Rüdesheim, Hattenheim, Steinberg/Kloster Eberbach, Rauenthal, Hochheim and Bensheim, the last in the Bergstrasse region and included only as a kind of appendage. Of these, only the large, entirely walled-in Steinberg estate is exclusively owned by the State. Also, the Research and Teaching Institute at Geisenheim, the oldest of its kind in Germany, holds an estate of larger size. In addition to the large holdings, there are a great many small ones and a number of excellent local growers' co-operatives; in one village, Hallgarten, there are even three of them. There are about 500 different sites in the Rheingau, a good many of them with famous names. Some localities and sites are situated immediately on the bank of the river, for others one has to walk two or three miles inland. It has also to be noted that the boundaries of some of the riverain towns extend far inland, so that some of their sites are as far from the river as are those of the upland villages.

The wines coming from the sites of Eltville (Sonnenberg, Kalbspflicht, etc.) are pleasing but not superlative in quality. To the west, Erbach is best known for its famous Marcobrunn site which extends as far as Hattenheim, but has in addition a number of sites owned by small producers. Hattenheim has a number of very good sites, such as Mannberg, Nussbrunnen, Wisselbrunn, Engelmannsberg, Bergweg, Pflänzer, etc.; higher up within its boundaries is also the Steinberg, too famous to display the name of Hattenheim on its labels. Further, Oestrich with Lenchen, Doosberg, etc.; Winkel with Schloss Vollrads, Hasensprung, etc.; Geisenheim with Morschberg, Hinkelstein, Rothenberg, etc. The town of Rüdesheim, at the foot of the very steep Rüdesheimer Berg, commands a great number of sites. Those situated on the face of this steep slope carry the word 'Berg' preceding their name, e.g., Berg Rottland, Berg Roseneck, Berg Lay, Berg

Bronnen, etc.; other Rüdesheim sites: Bischofsberg, Hinterhaus, etc. Indeed, Rüdesheim can boast of a great wealth of excellent wines, but it also happens to be the chief attraction of the local tourist trade. The more discerning wine-lover may be glad to give a wide berth to its Mecca, the Drosselgasse, a thoroughfare no more than seven feet wide, crammed with bustling crowds of holiday-makers—three million visitors a year—intent on finding room in one or other of the numerous wine-taverns for drinking and noisy merrymaking. Of the upland villages, Rauenthal (very misleadingly named, literally 'Rough Valley'), to the north of Eltville, sits on top of its vineyard sites, most of them rather steep. The best Rauenthal sites are undoubtedly in the top bracket of Rheingau wines. Rauenthal sites: Baiken, Gehrn, Wülfen, Burggraben, Pfaffenberg, Wieshell, etc., down to the more humble but still excellent Siebenmorgen and Kilbitzberg. Westwards, Kiedrich with its Wasserros, Gräfenberg, Sandgrub, etc.; Hallgarten with Hendelberg, Deutelsberg, Mehrhölzchen, Jungfer, Schönhell, etc.; Johannisberg with Schloss Johannisberg and the sites of Johannisberg village, Klaus, Hölle, Nonnenhöll, and others. The best-known local name, Erntebringer, is not that of a site but a so-called 'Gattungs-name' (generic name), which may be applied to wines grown within a wider radius. Hochheim, on the lower Main, has already been mentioned as giving its name to the English term 'Hock' (see above, p. 5). Although outside the Rheingau geographically, it is included in the Rheingau region because of the similar character of its wines. Hochheim sites: Domdechaney, Kirchenstück, Stein, Viktoriaberg, etc. Also included in the region, at its western end, is the so-called 'Lower Rheingau', the stretch from the northward bend of the river at the 'Binger Loch' (Bingen gorge) as far as Lorch, characterized by steep slate slopes like those of the adjoining Middle Rhine region farther north. The town of Assmannshausen, immediately to the north of the Bingen gorge, specializes in red wine, obtained exclusively from the Late Burgundy (Pinot noir) vine. By far the most important site is the steep Höllenberg with its purplish Taunus slate, owned by the

State Domain. The writer has tasted it both in the cellars of the local establishment and at the Eltville headquarters and agrees with the claim that it is the superior German red wine. His judgment would be half-way between that of S. F. Hallgarten and that of Rudolf Krämer-Badoni, the former writing in English, the latter in German, but both natives of the Rheingau and eminent connoisseurs. According to the former, 'Assmannshauser is a red wine, but no Burgundy'; according to the latter, it is 'today absolutely equivalent to Claret and Burgundy'. Between Assmannshausen and Lorchhausen, as has been said before, geography changes. The wines grown on the steep slaty slopes of this stretch belong to the Rheingau only officially; in character they are much the same as those of the Middle Rhine.

The fortunes of two monastic foundations in the Rheingau, Eberbach Abbey and Johannisberg Castle, both outstanding in the history of German viticulture, may be mentioned as examples of the vicissitudes brought about by the secularization. Both are situated in what at their time was the ecclesiastical Electorate of Mainz and were founded, in the early twelfth century, under the auspices of its Prince Archbishop. Eberbach was taken over by the Cistercians in 1135. Apart from the nearby Steinberg, which they made famous with their labours, they acquired and developed vineyard sites dispersed all over the Rheingau between Assmannshausen and Hochheim. Although badly ravaged in the wars of the sixteenth and seventeenth centuries, the monastery survived until its dissolution in the course of the secularization of 1803, when, with its entire vineyard property, it became a State Domain of the Duchy of Nassau. When the duchy was swallowed by Prussia in 1866, it became a Prussian Domain, and when Prussia disappeared from the map in 1945 it became a Domain of the reconstituted State of Hesse. Its present acreage, the largest centrally administered complex of vineyard estates in Germany, is believed to correspond approximately with that formerly held by the monastery.

Johannisberg's passage from ecclesiastical to secular ownership was more chequered. It was founded as a Benedictine Abbey in

1130, flourished during the following centuries but is said to have gradually declined in monastic discipline. In 1563 the monastery had to be dissolved, badly mauled by the upheavals of the previous decades, and the estate was run by a steward installed by the Archbishopric of Mainz. During the Thirty Years' War, it passed into the control of the Imperial Tax-collector as collateral security for a loan advanced to Mainz, subsequently changing over into the control of a Cologne banking-house. After a break of more than a century and a half, the Prince Abbot of Fulda acquired the estate by redeeming the mortgage and re-established the monastery as a Priory under the jurisdiction of the Benedictine Abbey of Fulda. The new monks restored the neglected vineyards successfully, planting them with Riesling vines and gradually improving the quality of their yield. On the dissolution of the monastery in the course of the secularization, the Prince of Orange became the next proprietor of the estate in 1803, but was soon relieved of it by Napoleon, who in 1807 gave it to his Marshal Kellermann, whom he had made Duke of Valmy. Kellermann could enjoy it only until 1813, when the Prussians approached. In 1815 it was given to the Emperor of Austria at the Congress of Vienna, who in turn presented it to his State Chancellor Prince Metternich, with the proviso, however, that a tithe of the annual yield should be paid to the head of the Imperial Dynasty or his legal successor. The present owner of Johannisberg Castle is the great-grandson in the male line of the Austrian statesman, and the present recipient of the tithe, in cash of course, is the great-great-great-nephew of the original one, Dr. Otto von Habsburg, who, being constitutionally barred from his native Austria as a security risk, consumes it in neighbouring Bavaria, where the hearts of monarchists beat for the House of Wittelsbach.

The Franconian region covers the middle course of the river Main and its tributaries, from about half-way between Bamberg and Schweinfurt in the east to half-way between Aschaffenburg and Hanau in the west. Within these limits, the river deviates from its general east-west direction in a series of erratic turns and bulges. At Schweinfurt it takes a plunge southward, skirting the western slopes of the Steigerwald range. At Ochsenfurt it describes the 'Main triangle' by turning north-west and flowing past Würzburg, the Franconian capital. At the apex of this north-western run, at Langenprozelten, after receiving the Franconian Saale, its main northern tributary, it begins the 'Main quadrangle' round the heavily wooded Spessart hills, first turning south again, changing to west at Urphar, being joined by the Tauber, its main southern tributary, at Wertheim, then turning north at Miltenberg and finally north-west after passing Aschaffenburg.

The soils of the region are, on the whole, rather heavy. Shell-lime predominates over the larger part of the region: on the right bank south of Schweinfurt, on both sides of the north-western course between Ochsenfurt and Langenprozelten as well as on the Franconian Saale, and again on the left bank southward about as far as Homburg or beyond. The soils above Schweinfurt and on the left bank of the southern course below it are predominantly red marl, which at the southern end of it, in the Iphofen area, is interspersed with gypsum layers. The inner side of the 'quadrangle', the slopes of the Spessart, is characterized by variegated sandstone soils. Finally, below Aschaffenburg, primary rock (mica-slate, gneiss and granite) takes over.

The following are some of the better-known wine-producing localities and sites. Escherndorf, with its sites Lump, Lämmerberg, etc., is situated on the right bank of the southward course below Schweinfurt; farther south on the same side Kitzingen and at the southern end of the 'Triangle' Frickenhausen. On the opposite side are Volkach, Sommerach, and farther south Iphofen with its site Julius-Echter-Berg, etc., Rödelsee and Abtswind. On the north-west run, Randersacker, with its sites Pfülben, Spielberg, Hohbug, etc., enjoys a reputation for the outstanding quality of its products. From here it is only about three miles to Würzburg, the centre of the local wine-trade and seat of the central administration of the Bavarian State Domains. Extending at considerable length to the north of the city is the Steinberg, or Stein, a ridge with an uninterrupted juxtaposition of separately named vineyard slopes, all facing south or south-south-east. The name 'Steinwein', properly applicable only to these sites, is often wrongly extended to the wines of the whole region, making 'Steinwein' synonymous with 'Frankenwein'. On the other side of the river, the Feste Marienberg—the palace fortress of the former Prince Bishops—is perched on top of a very steep hill, the slopes of which produce the Leiste wines, milder and more delicate than those of the Stein, and at their best when coming from the south slope, the 'Innere Leiste'. Downstream from Würzburg is Thüngersheim, with sites Johannisberg, Ravensburg, Scharlach, etc. Situated on the left bank of the second southward stretch is Homburg with its site Kallmuth which produces one of the best-known Franconian wines. On the northward stretch of the river, on the western slope of the Spessart hills, Klingenberg specializes in red wines, and Hörstein, at the western end of the region, in Riesling cultivation.

The visitor to Franconia would do well to spend a few days in Würzburg,[14] if only to sample the wines of the region at the proper places, the cellars of the Residence of the former Prince Bishops, now owned by the Administration of the State Domains, and the large taverns annexed to two old charitable institutions, the Juliusspital, founded by Prince Bishop Julius Echter von Mespelbrunn in 1576, and the Bürgerspital zum Heiligen Geist, founded as a home for old people by wealthy citizens in 1319.

Half of the total production of the region consists of Silvaner, while the proportion of the Müller-Thurgau variety is variously recorded as thirty or thirty-eight per cent. Silvaner generally yields better wines on shell-lime, the most widely found kind of soil, than on red marl soils, while variegated sandstone and primary rock soils are unsuitable for it. It is at its best on sites where the shell-lime basis is covered with a fertile layer of loess, as, e.g., at Randersacker, Escherndorf, and some other places. Generally, Franconian Silvaners are full-bodied, dry and earthy; they may have more of a delicate bouquet than Silvaners elsewhere. The red marl soils of the upper reaches of the river and the gypsum-red marl soils of the Iphofen area are more suitable for Müller-Thurgau and two more recent crossings between Riesling and

Silvaner: Rieslaner and Scheurebe, as well as for the frost-resistant Perle vine, a crossing between Gewürztraminer and Müller-Thurgau. Only between three and four per cent of the total production consists of Riesling. It is planted on the best plots of the Würzburg sites Stein and Leiste, on certain sites at Randersacker and Escherndorf and on the Kallmuth site of Homburg. All these sites have shell-lime soils and produce predominantly Silvaner. Some Riesling is also grown on the Julius-Echterberg site at Iphofen, on gypsum-red marl soil. Owing to the prevailing heavy soils, all these Rieslings, though richer in bouquet than the Silvaners, share the typical character of the Franconian wines; moreover, they mature only in the best years. The only Franconian Riesling that grows on really suitable soil, namely, primary rock, and is therefore quite different and attractive, comes from the extreme western end of the region, especially from the Abtsberg and Reuschberg sites of Hörstein. The area is well protected against harsh north and east winds by the heights of the Spessart, and seems on the whole to be more favoured climatically than most other parts of the region. Red wine of the Late Burgundy variety comes mostly from the steep variegated sandstone slopes of Klingenberg. Virtually all Franconian wines grow on slopes, often enough very steep ones. All the white ones, at least ninety-seven per cent of the total, are bottled in flasks of a distinctive shape known as 'Bocksbeutel' (literally, 'he-goat scrotum'); for those who are not familiar with it, the flask of the Portuguese Mateus Rosé has a similar shape.

The subject of 'Frankenwein' is, frankly, more controversial than that of any other German wine. The region has two natural disadvantages: most of it is situated still farther east than is Württemberg, that is, has a more continental climate with shorter summers and harder winters, and, secondly, its soils are generally heavy. Other arguments are more matters of taste. Most wine-lovers would probably say that Silvaner is not the top-ranking German variety. The Franconian locals would probably answer that they prefer a solid, full-bodied, dry and earthy Silvaner to the fancy airy fragrance of a Riesling; and good luck to them.

There may also be some truth in the claim that Franconian wine is not much mucked about, is generally 'naturrein' and 'durchgegoren' (fermented right through). This claim is sometimes pressed a little too far in the assertion that Franconian wine is 'honest', which seems to imply the charge that dishonesty is the common characteristic of all other German wines. One is also constantly reminded, in speech and print, that Goethe preferred Franconian wines, and especially his beloved Echerndorfer, to any others. This is quite true, but as a claim to superiority the argument falls flat when one considers that a hundred and fifty or more years ago Franconian wine, like Rheingau or any other German wine, was something entirely different from the highly developed and sophisticated wines of today. Local wine patriotism, or wine parochialism, exists in all wine-growing regions, but Franconia seems to have received a double dose of it. Nowhere do local people seem to be more touchy about their wines, to protest too much; nowhere does the outsider get a stronger impression that the alleged superiority is more an ideology than a fact. It seems quite possible that the local propaganda may persuade people in northern Germany (who know no more about German wines than do people in this country) to mend their ways and drink more 'honest' Franconian wine. But is it likely that a non-German connoisseur could ever wax as enthusiastic about Franconian wines as Frank Schoonmaker did about Rheingau wines?

As has been emphasized before, the Riesling wines of Lorch and Lorchhausen, though officially classified as Rheingau products, are essentially of the same character as those of the Middle Rhine region farther down the river. The main wine-growing localities on the left bank are Bacharach, together with Steeg which is situated in a side valley, Oberwesel, St. Goar and Boppard; on the right bank, Lorchhausen, Kaub, St. Goarshausen, Braubach and Ehrenbreitstein (opposite Koblenz); at the northern end, Königswinter, at the foot of the Siebengebirge, is exceptional in producing a red Portugieser named 'Drachenblut' (dragon's blood), apparently mainly for the benefit of tourists. Generally, vineyards are mostly terraced high up on breakneck slopes of meagre slate. Quite a few wine-growing villages are situated still higher up in the hills, above their vineyards. Above Koblenz, Riesling reigns supreme, but only in relative quantity. The spectacular beauty of this part of the Rhine valley is well known, but its wines do not measure up to it. They are, by and large, modest table-wines, mostly grown for local consumption; what is left over is not enough to quench the thirst of the tourist swarms. Even from the best sites and the best vintages, there is nothing that can be compared to a good Rheingau wine. There are obviously natural deficiencies, whether of soil or climate or both, but German sources are remarkably tight-lipped about the causes of the 'underprivileged' nature of Middle Rhine wines. Three hundred years ago, Bacharach was widely famed for its wines; but it is questionable whether the wines going under its name were of local growth or even from anywhere near. It seems much more likely that the town was only the distribution centre for wines coming from far higher up the river.

In one of the most recent statistics of the German Wine-growers' Association (August, 1969), Bergstrasse wines are registered as a separate region, with a total production equalling that of the Middle Rhine; previously those of the northern half were classified as Hesse wines, a kind of appendix to those of the Rheingau, and those of the southern half as Baden wines. The Bergstrasse runs along the western foothills of the densely wooded Odenwald. Separated by the very wide Rhine plain, the northern half of the region is situated opposite Rhine-Hesse, its southern half opposite the Palatinate. Soils are pretty variable, but in the main clayey, calcareous soils of marl, sporadically also loess-loam. Wine-growing places extend from Zwingenberg in the north to Wiesloch in the south; the latter place, situated about 10 miles south of Heidelberg, is not on the Odenwald slopes and therefore not part of the Bergstrasse geographically, but is classified as such in the official statistics of Baden. The main wine-growing localities are, in Hesse: Bensheim, Schönberg (in a side valley nearby), and Heppenheim; in Baden: Laudenbach, Weinheim, Schriesheim,

Dossenheim, Heidelberg, Leimen and Wiesloch. Vineyard properties are mostly small, and most of the wines grown are consumed locally. The Bergstrasse certainly cannot be said to produce 'great' wines; they are, in general, lighter and less full-bodied than those of the Rheingau, Rhine-Hesse and the Palatinate, yet they are pleasantly fresh. Riesling wines represent less than a quarter of the total production; those coming from the sites of the Hesse State Domain at Bensheim, Schönberg and Heppenheim, and again those grown on a patch of porphyry soil at Weinheim in Baden, as well as some of the Rieslings grown farther south, at Schriesheim, Leimen and Wiesloch, are quite respectable representatives of the variety. Schriesheim produces a Silvaner that stands up to any good Palatinate Silvaner. Ruländer, now grown in most Bergstrasse communities, is not on a par with that of the Kaiserstuhl, from where its cultivation was first introduced. A little to the south of Weinheim, two villages, Lützelsachsen and Grosssachsen, grow Late Burgundy red wine on the variegated sandstone of their area.

Finally, the smallest of the German regions, also the most northerly, that of the little river Ahr, which rises in the Eifel plateau and joins the Rhine between Remagen and Sinzig. Viticulture is confined to the lower twenty-five miles of the river's course. The Ahr valley is often called 'the German red-wine paradise'. It is indeed, in spite of its small size, the largest continuous red-wine producing area; everywhere else red-wine cultivation is more sporadic. At the same time, it is not exclusively preoccupied with red-wine cultivation; official statistics register a white-wine production of no less than forty per cent of the total. The wine-producing places are Kreuzberg, Altenahr, Mayschoss, Rech, Dernau, Marienthal, Walporzheim, Bachem, Ahrweiler, Neuenahr, and Bodendorf. The valley is extremely narrow, with rocks closely pressed together intensifying the summer heat by reflection and mists rising up from the river warming the night-air. Yet in spite of such natural advantages there can be few places where the grower's labour is as strenuous as in the Ahr region, at least in the greater part of its length. Tiny terraced vineyard plots have to be constructed on precipitous slopes high up above the valley bottom, entirely out of reach for any kind of viticultural machinery; black broken-up slate has to be laboriously carried up to provide a heat-absorbing topsoil. There are said to be two thousand smallholders, with an average individual holding of one and a quarter acre, and that mostly fragmented in tiny bits and pieces; and they are served by fifteen growers' co-operatives. The reputation of the Ahr is based on its Late Burgundy; actually, more Portugieser is grown on the more accessible lower reaches of the slopes. A great deal of praise is showered on the Late Burgundy; in great years it certainly has good quality and may be both fiery and velvety. But the assertion that it can bear comparison with foreign red wines, or even the recurring story that wily French connoisseurs often cannot tell the Late Burgundy of the Ahr from their own Burgundies seem to be going just a little too far. Probably a greater number of German red-wine lovers would consider the Ahr Late Burgundy a smaller wine than that from Assmannshausen, or Affenthal, or some other place in Baden. The visitor who wants to use his own judgment in the rating of German Late Burgundies locally may be warned to avoid the Ahr on weekends, when vast noisy hordes from the cities of the lower Rhine and the Ruhr infest the place.

7. The New German Wine Law

The new law, passed on 19th July, 1969, and coming into force on the same date two years later, has already been briefly mentioned (see above, p. 35). Its raisons d'être are innovations in cultivation methods and cellar technology, general economic changes and, last not least, the competitiveness of German viticulture within the EEC. The following are only a few of the novel features distinguishing it from the previous law of 1930.[15]

The core of the new law is the classification of German wines in three main categories, *viz.*, 'Tischwein' (table-wine), 'Qualitätswein', and 'Qualitätswein mit Prädikat' (with predicate, that is, special quality designation, see above, p. 35ff). Every label has to carry the one or other of these terms. (We shall refer to them briefly as Table-wine, Quality-wine, and Predicate-wine.) The conditions imposed become increasingly stricter from the first to the third category, both in respect of the initial natural must gravity demanded and in the narrowing designation of geographical origin. The latter condition refers not only to the main categories, but also to a scale of subdivisions within them.

As has already been pointed out (see above, p. 34f), terms expressing or implying that a wine is natural (unsugared), such as 'Natur', 'naturrein', 'Naturwein', 'Wachstum', 'Original-abfüllung', etc., are in future banned from labels. A Table-wine is likely to be sugared, and sugaring is also allowed in the Quality category. It is permitted to a limited extent, the limits being narrower than in the old law; moreover, it may be done only in the region of origin. What may seem puzzling to the outsider is that the limits are wider in respect of the period within which it is allowed: in the old law it had to be done before the 31st of January following the grape-harvest, while the new law extends it to the 31st of March. It is only in the Predicate category, without exception, that wines must be natural, that is, unsugared. Thus, if the consumer wants to be certain of an unsugared wine, he has to buy a bottle marked 'Cabinet' (or 'Kabinett'), 'Spätlese', 'Auslese', 'Beerenauslese', 'Trockenbeerenauslese', or 'Eiswein', the choice being determined by how much he cares to spend on it.

Wines of both the Quality and the Predicate classes must be from approved kinds of vine; they must be faultless in appearance, flavour and taste, and they must be typical of the character of the region as well as of the kind of vine indicated on the label.

There is a novelty introduced by the new law, namely, the notion of a 'Bereich' (environs). The term denotes a complex of several named 'Lagen' (sites, see above, p. 30f), either within the boundaries of a single local community or extending beyond them into a neighbouring community, or neighbouring communities, but in any case producing wines of the same general character. The number of site names is legion and therefore very bewildering to the consumer, as well as being a handicap to the sale of German wines. The introduction of this notion promises at least a beginning in cleaning up the vast clutter of baffling site names. However, the new environs names are still to be agreed upon and laid down. Moreover, their introduction does not mean the general abolishment of site names but only their reduction, in so far as that in future they are to be reserved for the Quality and Predicate categories.

The narrowing strictures in the designations of geographical origin can best be seen in their relation to the regulation of blendings. Only in the Table-wine category is inter-regional blending allowed; for example, a Moselle wine may be blended with one from the Palatinate, etc. The widest geographical designation, permissible only for this category, indicates only its German origin, thus, e.g., 'Deutscher Weisswein'. In the absence of a regional designation, it may, in this case, be assumed that the wine is a blend made up from wines of two or more regions and that none of the parts contributed by a single region reaches seventy-five or more per cent of the total. The label will give a fancy name, the choice of which must not be suggestive of any real site name. If in the inter-regional blend one particular region has contributed seventy-five or more per cent, the wine is one rung higher up the ladder and may go under the name of that region, thus, e.g., 'Rheinhessen'. However, it will still be known by a fancy name. If, in addition to the regional name, the label bears a wider local designation after the word 'Bereich' (environs), at least seventy-five per cent of the blend must come from the named environs. Lastly, if it bears the name of a village or town, at least seventy-five per cent must come from within the boundaries of that particular local community. It is important to note that on this highest step of the Table-wine category inter-regional blending is no longer allowed; that is, the rest of the blend must come from the same region. Site names are not permitted within the whole of the Table-wine category. Thus, if one sees a site name following a local name on a label, it indicates that the wine is at least in the Quality category, which, incidentally, is also made explicit on the label.

The crucial seventy-five per cent limitation, in the Table-wine category, applies also to the indication of the vintage year and of the kind of vine; at least seventy-five per cent of the blend must come from the particular year and the particular vine.

The widest geographical designation in the Quality category is that of a single region, meaning that in blends all portions must originate from the same region, as in the top class of the Table-wine category. In the Predicate category the widest geographical designation is that of a single environs, meaning again that if there is any blending all parts must come from the same environs. As the narrowest geographical designation, the names of sites are strictly reserved for Quality and Predicate wines only. Thus, it can be seen that, in the regulation of geographical designations, there is an overlap between the three categories.

8. Modernization

BESIDES destructive pests (see above, p. 29), there are, of course, also economic problems, such as the increasing consumption of imported wines, and still more the increasing beer consumption, which have contributed to the reduction of German wine-production. In competition with the much cheaper production in France and the Mediterranean countries, German viticulture can, in the long run, hold its own only if it produces wines of high quality, and at the same time succeeds in lowering production costs substantially by modernization and extensive mechanization. Qualitative improvement by scientific experimentation and generally setting an example to wine-growers is the main object of the so-called 'State domains', or estates owned and run by the respective Land, which are found in all wine-growing regions and are normally headed by men of outstanding ability and experience. They usually work in close association with viticultural or oenological (oenology, the more comprehensive term, means the science of wine-making, from the Greek *oinos*, wine) research and teaching institutes, some of them dating back to the late nineteenth century, at which prospective wine-growers receive a scientific training in all branches of the subject. Such colleges are situated at Geisenheim in the Rheingau, Trier and Bernkastel-Kues for the Moselle region, Bad Kreuznach for the Nahe region, Oppenheim in Rhine-Hesse, Neustadt an der Weinstrasse Siebeldingen and Speyer in the Palatinate, Weinsberg near Heilbronn for Württemberg, Freiburg im Breisgau for

Baden, Veitshöchheim near Würzburg for Franconia (northern Bavaria), and Ahrweiler for the Ahr region.

Wine-growers' co-operatives made their first appearance during the second half of the nineteenth century. Today, the co-operative system plays a highly important part in wine-production. At present, there exist about five hundred and fifty local co-operatives, accounting for nearly a third of the total production. Initially, it was mainly the concern for the sale of their produce that caused growers to form associations, However, with the modernization of viticulture, and great demands made by consumers, the raison d'être of co-operatives has undergone some change. The smallholder cannot afford the modern wine-presses and other complicated and expensive equipment indispensable for the proper cellar treatment of wine—often enough, he does not even have a cellar of his own. There is, broadly speaking, a division of labour between grower and co-operative. The former takes care of the vine almost throughout the year, an arduous enough task at the best of times even with modern labour-saving devices. As soon as he has delivered the harvested grapes in the cellar, the co-operative with its trained staff takes over, developing and finally selling the wine. The co-operative system seems to be most highly organized in Baden, in accordance with that country's predominant smallholding structure. The visitor will receive a strong impression of its efficiency in the little cathedral city of Breisach, south of the Kaiserstuhl hills, which houses the Central Cellarage of the Baden Wine-growers' Co-operatives, an enterprise including the most up-to-date equipment and modern giant tanks with a total capacity of forty million litres (Plate 11).

The trend towards modernization and rationalization of production is perhaps best exemplified by what may be its most radical means, namely, the restructuring and consolidation of the entire viticultural acreage of a locality, mostly referred to by the term 'Flurbereinigung'. In general, this does not apply to the larger properties which are mostly continuous wholes to begin with. But most of the smaller holdings are, traditionally, by way of inheritance through generations, fragmented into a number of small and often widely scattered patches, often difficult of access, and interspersed with similar parcels of other holdings—a situation that contradicts economic sense. The remedy consists in redivision, an exchange of plots, the merging of several adjacent plots into new units, with the result that the individual smallholder gains an undivided larger piece of land; that narrow, steep and often impassable field-paths can be replaced with suitably graded vineyard roads, and that cultivation can be intensified by mechanization. Naturally, since plots are unequal in productive value and often also have a sentimental value to their owners, the process requires a good deal of patience and more than simple persuasion, involving compensation or payment, and above all, government aid. Moreover, there are topographical limits set to it, especially as regards machinery, as everybody can see who looks at the steep slopes of the Middle Rhine, the Moselle, the Ahr and the Main. At any rate, the process of an economically viable redivision and reallocation of vineyard sites has only begun after the last war and is as yet far from completion.

9. Choosing from a Wine-list

THE TRUE wine-lover will usually put the wine before the food, choosing a wine for its own sake and food as incidental to the drinking. But wine is also an important accompaniment of a good meal, and there should be harmony between the food and the wine. There is nothing wrong with serving the same carefully chosen and well-balanced wine throughout the whole meal; indeed, too much fussiness in trying to find the right wine for the right dish might easily seem to smack a little of wine-snobbery. However, as a general rule, if different wines are to be served, the sequence should be from the light and fresh with the hors-d'oeuvres and fish via the full-bodied with the main courses to the high-quality wine at the end of the meal.

When travelling in Germany, a wine of the district will generally be chosen, and the advice of the landlord or restaurateur is worth taking, because he will know the characteristics of each vintage in his cellar. German wine-books or pamphlets tend to advise the novice, as a basic rule, that white wine should go with white meat, and red with dark meat. But there are regions without local reds, or good local reds; and anyway there is no dish in the recommended red-wine category for which an appropriate white wine would not be equally satisfactory.

The following recommendations are necessarily tentative, since obviously not all the wines noted are available everywhere. Nevertheless, they may be helpful in a general way, inasmuch as particular suggestions may easily be modified by the choice of appropriate local substitutes.

Hors-d'oeuvres of all kinds: a crisp tingling Riesling from the Moselle, Saar, Ruwer, or from the Nahe. Boiled or stewed fish: a light fruity Riesling, or a Gutedel from southern Baden, etc. Salmon: a full-flavoured Riesling from the Rheingau, Rhine-Hesse, the Palatinate or the Ortenau (Baden). Asparagus: the same. Fried white meat (veal, pork, lamb, chicken): a full-bodied Traminer or Ruländer from Baden or the Palatinate. Cold meat plate, ham and savouries: a dry robust wine, perhaps a Silvaner, from Franconia or the Palatinate.

The following dishes may, but need not, be accompanied by red wine. Fried or smoked fish, as well as grilled meat and game birds (quail, partridge, pheasant): a light and mild red wine, e.g., Frühburgunder (Early Burgundy). Venison with more marked gamy flavour (hare, deer, red deer, wild boar): a full-bodied Spät-burgunder (Late Burgundy), or, especially in Baden, perhaps a Weissherbst (Rosé). Dark meat (roast beef, mutton, turkey, goose, duck): a heavy, full-bodied Late Burgundy. Pâté de foie gras: a top-quality Late Burgundy. Cheese: a fruity Late Burgundy or, in Württemberg, a robust Trollinger.

The proper accompaniment of sweet desserts is, if anything, coffee, certainly not wine.

Some advice on the age of wines, and on vintages generally, may not be out of place. On the whole, current taste favours younger wines. The fond belief that age invariably improves the quality of a wine—the older the better—is a myth. Every wine, even the best, has its life-span, reaches its optimal maturity at a certain age and then gradually falls off. The German expression for a wine that has passed its prime is "firn", meaning flat or stale.

The most important criteria for the choice of a wine are: the kind of grape from which it is made (discussed in the chapter on Vines), the region from which it comes (characterized in that on the Wine-growing Regions), and lastly the vintage year. Since climatic conditions may differ in different regions, only the most summary survey of post-war vintages can be given.

Vintages of outstanding quality were 1945, 1947 and 1949, but for all practical purposes they remain only as a lingering in some wine-lovers' memory. 1953 produced a first-rate vintage, but little of it seems to be left apart from a few bottles of exquisite Beerenauslese or Trockenbeerenauslese, costing anything between DM100 and more than DM200 each. The extraordinary 1959 vintage has rightly been called "the wine of the century", but most of what remains is likely to have turned stale by now. 1960—In spite of a record quantity, these wines, generally of medium quality, have almost disappeared from the market. 1961—A small vintage with a few memorable top-quality wines, virtually unobtainable now. 1962—Varying qualities, still occasionally on offer. 1963—Good yield of generally medium quality, still to be found on many price-lists. 1964—Very good vintage with large yield and a considerable range of quality, but some of its wines already past their prime. 1965—Fresh and fruity wines with hardly any top qualities, becoming rare. 1966—A comparatively small vintage, generally above average with many top-quality wines. 1967—A good vintage with considerable range of quality. 1968—Generally below average, with few high-quality wines. 1969—A good vintage, generally above average and with many top-quality wines. 1970—The largest quantity of the present century, some say, since the Thirty Years' War,—with presumably generally more-than-average qualities.

𝕹otes

(1) The following chart shows the increasing yields, in hectolitres, of post-war vintages.

Vintage	Quantity	Vintage	Quantity
1945 . . .	. *c.* 508 000	1958 . . .	. 4 800 000
1946 . . .	*c.* 1 239 000	1959 . . .	. 4 303 000
1947 . . .	. 1 150 000	1960 . . .	. 7 433 000
1948 . . .	. 2 186 000	1961 . . .	. 3 574 000
1949 . . .	. 1 363 000	1962 . . .	. 3 928 000
1950 . . .	. 3 247 000	1963 . . .	. 6 034 000
1951 . . .	. 3 114 000	1964 . . .	. 7 185 000
1952 . . .	. 2 715 000	1965 . . .	. 5 035 000
1953 . . .	. 2 457 000	1966 . . .	. 4 809 000
1954 . . .	. 3 100 000	1967 . . .	. 6 069 000
1955 . . .	. 2 408 000	1968 . . .	. 6 048 000
1956 . . .	. 930 000	1969 . . .	. 5 947 000
1957 . . .	. 2 264 000	1970*	

* A bumper crop exceeding any previous harvest in living memory.

(2) According to a brochure entitled 'Deutschland und seine Weine', a special edition of the 'Deutsche Weinkorrespondenz', 1966, Germany produces 80 hectolitres (1760 gallons) per hectare (=2·47 acres), France 40·8 hectolitres (897 gallons), Italy 37 (814 gallons).

(3) According to a brochure entitled 'Deutscher Weinatlas', by Rudi vom Endt, annual consumption in France is 130 litres, in Italy 115, in Portugal 70, in Spain 52, in Greece 41, in Switzerland 37, in Luxemburg 35, in Yugoslavia 20, in Austria 20, in Germany 16.

(4) The omission of the Germans may be significant. As to the Britons, viticulture in Roman times would be probable on the face of it, but archaeological evidence seems to be scanty. However, for post-Roman times we have the explicit evidence of the Venerable Bede for vineyards in England as well as in Ireland, and a law issued by Alfred the Great laying down a penalty for the offence of damaging another man's 'wîngeard'. Other Anglo-Saxon compounds: wînberige (wine-berry), wînclyster (grape-cluster), wîngeardnaem (grape-harvest).

It is probably well known that some small-scale and more or less sportive viticulture is being carried on in Hampshire, Surrey and probably elsewhere in the south of England. See Ray Barrington Brock: *Outdoor Grapes in Cold Climates*, 1949; *Progress with Vines and Wines*, 1961; *Vineyards in England* (Faber and Faber); Edwards Hyams: *The Grapevine in England* (Bodley Head). An old book should not be forgotten, Alexander Henderson's *The History of Ancient and Modern Wines*, 1824, which refers, for example, to an apparently extensive cultivation in the Vale of Gloucester in the twelfth century as well as to more sportive attempts to revive viticulture in the eighteenth century.

(5) These and other names, referring to large tribal aggregates, appear for the first time in the third century.

(6) See Anthony Rich: *A Dictionary of Roman and Greek Antiquities*, 4th ed., 1874, articles Calcator and Calcatorium (p. 98), Torcular and Torcularium (pp. 673–677), with several illustrations. The writer is indebted for this reference to Dr. David Smith, Keeper of the Museum of Antiquities, University of Newcastle upon Tyne.

(7) 'Primus botrus in torculari pressus est Christus'. The sentence is more mystical than grammatical. In latinizing the Greek word for a bunch of grapes, the Church Father changes its gender from feminine to masculine.

(8) A brochure entitled 'Weinbau heute und morgen', published in 1969 by the Secretary General of the German Wine-growers' Association, Dr. Werner Becker.

(9) The reader who would like to have more detailed information should consult the books by Alfred Langenbach and S. F. Hallgarten mentioned in the preface.

(10) These data have been culled from an article entitled 'Das neue deutsche Weingesetz' by Dr. Werner Becker. The present writer greatly regrets that, when writing this chapter, he was unaware of the existence of a little booklet entitled *German Wine Law* 1969 by S. F. Hallgarten, published by Harper Trade Journals Ltd. (94 pp., price 25p). Dr. Hallgarten discusses the question more thoroughly, also taking up a number of points which Dr. Becker's short article does not raise, for example, the insertion of the new notion of 'Grosslage' (grand site) between those of 'Lage' and 'Bereich'. There is, however, one point which he does not seem to have considered, namely, the very drastic provision that a site-name may be entered into the new vineyard-register only if the site covers at least 5 hectares. This, of course, relegates legions of old site-names to limbo, and in so far as they are entirely superfluous and only confusing, good riddance. But there are a good many smaller sites whose names have, over the last hundred or more years, helped to build up the international

reputation of German wines. To give only one of many examples, the famous Bernkasteler Doctor comes from a site measuring only 1⅓ hectares. Such cases seem to be taken care of by a clause to the general provision admitting exceptions from the 5 hectares rule 'if the formation of a larger site is not possible because of the local conditions of utilization or because of the singularity (Besonderheit) of the wines gained from the surface'. So one may hope that the really outstanding site-names may be saved from oblivion. However, as a general impression the writer is still, a year and a half later, inclined to agree with Dr. Hallgarten's view (p. 16) that 'the wine-law as it is now is not complete', and furthermore, he suspects that also the German wine pundits themselves are still not as yet entirely out of the dark.

(11) The reader who wishes for more comprehensive information should consult the books by Frank Schoonmaker, Alfred Langenbach and S. F. Hallgarten mentioned in the preface. The last of these is especially recommended for the detail it gives on the composition of soils in different regions, a highly important determinant for the character of their wines.

(12) The table—p. 86—referring to the harvest of 1968, has been reproduced from the publication mentioned in note 8.

(13) This is the oldest of its kind in Germany, consisting of the former vineyard estates of the Prince Bishops of Konstanz, which in the course of the secularization were taken over by the Crown of Baden in 1802 and managed by the subsequently established state domain administration since 1812.

(14) German Wines, p. 77.

(15) The city, one of the most beautiful examples of Baroque architecture in Germany, was almost completely wiped out by the RAF in the night of 16th March, 1945, more than a month after Dresden, but has been reconstructed as well as humanly possible.

	Must harvest in hectolitres	Productive vine surface in hectares	Percentage of main varieties in vine	
Palatinate	1 700 000	18 212	Silvaner M.-Thurgau Portugieser Riesling	35 23 16 14
Rhine-Hesse	1 500 000	16 373	Silvaner M.-Thurgau Portugieser Riesling	41 36 7 6
Moselle–Saar–Ruwer	900 000	10 153	Riesling M.-Thurgau Elbling	77 12 11
Baden	700 000	8 334	M.-Thurgau Late Burgundy Ruländer Gutedel Silvaner Riesling	27 22 13 13 7 7
Württemberg	460 000	6 375	Trollinger Riesling Silvaner Portugieser M.-Thurgau Limberger	27 23 12 11 6 6
Nahe	240 000	3 039	Silvaner M.-Thurgau Riesling	33 28 27
Rheingau	210 000	3 069	Riesling M.-Thurgau Silvaner	77 12 8
Franconia	120 000	2 322	Silvaner M.-Thurgau Riesling	48 38 4
Middle Rhine	70 000	976	Riesling M.-Thurgau Silvaner	85 8 4
Bergstrasse	70 000	830	M.-Thurgau Riesling Silvaner	36 23 17
Ahr	30 000	531	Portugieser Late Burgundy Riesling M.-Thurgau	31 24 23 17

STEIGERWALD
FRANCONIA
Fränk-Saale
WÜRZBURG
Tauber
Jagst
Kocher
Heilbro
SPESSART
Main
Neckar
W Ü
Aschaffenburg
ODENWALD
Heidelberg
KRAI
Weinheim
Bensheim
BERGSTRASSE
MANNHEIM
FRANKFURT
Darmstadt
LUDWIGSHAFEN
Speyer
TAUNUS
Hochheim
WORMS
PALATINATE
MAINZ
RHINE-
HARDT
WIESBADEN
RHEINGAU
Selz
HESSE
Neustadt/Weinstrasse
Bingen
Rüdesheim
Nahe
NAHE
Bad Kreuznach
SOON-
WALD
Lahn
Middle Rhine
Glan
UPP
MIDDLE RHINE
KOBLENZ
Moselle
HUNSRÜCK
AHR
Ahr
MOSELLE
Bernkastel-
Kues
SAARBRÜCKEN
RUWER
Ruwer
EIFEL
TRIER
SAAR
Saar